GUN SHOW NATION

GUN SHOW NATION

GUN CULTURE AND AMERICAN DEMOCRACY

JOAN BURBICK

THE NEW PRESS

NEW YORK
LONDON

Requests for permission to reproduce selections from this book should
be mailed to: Permissions Department, The New Press, 38 Greene Street,
New York, NY 10013.

Published in the United States by The New Press, New York, 2006
Distributed by W. W. Norton & Company, Inc., New York

LIBRARY OF CONGRESS CATALOGING-IN-PUBLICATION DATA

Burbick, Joan.
    Gun show nation : gun culture and American democracy / Joan Burbick.
        p.   cm.
    Includes bibliographical references and index.
    ISBN-13: 978-1-59558-087-0 (hc.)
    ISBN-10: 1-59558-087-5 (hc.)
        1. Gun control—United States—History.   2. Firearms ownership—
United States—History.   3. Firearms—Law and legislation—United
States—History.   4. Firearms—Social aspects—United States.   I. Title.
    HV7436.B87 2006
    363.330973—dc22

                                                        2006044415

The New Press was established in 1990 as a not-for-profit alternative to the
large, commercial publishing houses currently dominating the book publishing industry. The New Press operates in the public interest rather than for
private gain, and is committed to publishing, in innovative ways, works of
educational, cultural, and community value that are often deemed insuffi-
ciently profitable.

www.thenewpress.com

Composition by NK Graphics
This book was set in Fairfield LH Light

Printed in the United States of America

10   9   8   7   6   5   4   3   2   1

for Alex

*He who loves the bristle of bayonets only sees in their glitter
what beforehand he feels in his heart.*
—Ralph Waldo Emerson, "War"

*The public then supposed, as foreigners did and as still is the
case now with the mass of our people, that the American
people were a nation of riflemen. The Civil War, however,
showed very clearly the contrary.*
—George W. Wingate,
"The Development of
the Modern Rifle"

*Fondling their weapons, feeling suddenly so young and good
they are reminded that guns are more than decoration,
intimidation or comfort. They are meant.*
—Toni Morrison, *Paradise*

CONTENTS

ACKNOWLEDGMENTS

No book finds its way into the world without a web of support from family, friends, and colleagues. First, I would like to thank the people who talked with me at gun rights meetings and gun shows, and the dozen individuals who agreed to discuss their ideas and experiences with the gun rights movement during confidential interviews. I would also like to thank the Rockefeller Foundation that provided me with a residency at the Bellagio Study and Conference Center in Italy. The international group of scholars and artists present when I was working on this manuscript raised key questions as I was thinking through these ideas. In particular, I would like to thank Gianna Celli, Penelope Andrews, Tamar Hermann, Michael Honey, Ana Solari, Gail and Stephen Wight, and Douglas and Sharon Wilson. I would also like to thank Knox College in

Galesburg, Illinois, for providing me with office and library support in the spring of 2004 when I was the Distinguished Scholar-in-Residence on their campus, especially Vice President for Academic Affairs and Dean of the College Lawrence Breitborde and faculty members Lori Haslem, Robin Metz, and Elizabeth Carlin Metz.

Washington State University also supported my research and writing by granting me a professional leave during the academic year 2003–2004. And several faculty members working on masculinities in the Gender Research Across Curriculum (GRACe) study group have read sections of this book, specifically Lilian Ackerman, Faith Lutze, Jeannette Mageo, Heather Streets, and Noel Sturgeon. I would also like to thank Sue Armitage, Richard Slotkin, and Eric Sundquist for their ongoing support of my research. In addition, the 2005 conference at the Stanford Law School entitled "Gun Control: Old Problems, New Paradigms," sponsored by the Stanford Criminal Justice Center, the Stanford Law School, the Second Amendment Research Center and the Glenn Institute at the Ohio State University, was an opportunity to present and discuss my research and writing with lawyers, historians, public health policy makers, criminologists, and anthropologists, studying the many ways guns affect our lives in the United States. Portions of this book also appeared in "The Cultural Anatomy of a Gun Show," *Stanford Law and Policy Review*, forthcoming 2006, and with the editorial support of Mark Trahant and Kimberly Mills in "The Greatest Political Weapon There Is," *Seattle Times/Post-Intelligencer*, June 6, 2004.

I also would like to thank my editor, Marc Favreau, who stayed the course and kept my voice from wandering too far afield by understanding what I was trying to say. His efforts, his assistant Melissa Richards's, and those of the staff at The New

Press have made this journey much less arduous than it could have been.

A smart and challenging family also walks these pages. Special thanks to my brother, Stephen Burbick; brother-in-law, George Elsener; daughter, Claire Huntsberry; stepson, Stephen Kuo; and husband, Alex Kuo; thank you is clearly not enough. Nothing worth doing can be done without care.

INTRODUCTION

Political theater thrives on flashy stage props. In April of 2004, as the vice president of the United States, Dick Cheney, held a flintlock rifle in his hands at the National Rifle Association's annual convention in Pittsburgh, the cavernous ballroom shook with deafening applause. A gift from the NRA, the rifle was no bad-ass military weapon from *Rambo* movies. His flintlock was the honored gun of revolutionary patriots, the gun of our founding fathers, red-white-and-blue America. A long-time supporter of gun rights, Cheney, like the 3,000 NRA members in Convention Hall, was a freedom fighter, and they were celebrating a common heritage.

The vice president was there to address the NRA members, who had waited for hours to hear him speak. And he was there to bash his political opponent, John Kerry, the anticipated Democratic presidential candidate, who was in town on the same weekend. I listened to the joyful crowd cheer and shout each time he told them that President George W. Bush would protect their constitutional rights. Like rapt participants in a religious revival, many in the crowd nodded as Cheney reverently quoted from the Second Amendment to the Constitution: "the right of the people to keep and bear arms shall not be infringed." They cheered when told that only one candidate has "shown you respect," President Bush. Front-line patriots lining up to vote, they jeered at Kerry, chanting, "Four more years."

Guns entered our national politics with earnest in the 1960s, when the country was rocked by assassinations, dissent over the Vietnam War, and social change from the civil rights movement. Since then the political language of gun rights has only become louder and has found expression in several Second Amendment organizations, including the Institute for Legislative Action of the NRA. And organized gun owners have even pushed ahead of retired people in bringing their message and clout to Washington, D.C. In 2001, after the election of George W. Bush, the NRA topped the list of powerful Washington lobbies, edging ahead of the American Association of Retired Persons (AARP), according to *Fortune* magazine.[1]

Moreover, the success of this political language of gun rights only makes sense if we look back in time at how and when guns began to send political messages—and precisely who was able to send them and why. Without returning to this past, we are left with only a dim understanding of why since the 1960s our national politics have fostered endless conversations and debates about guns. As a writer and teacher of American culture at a state university and a woman who has lived in the rural West for almost thirty years, I have watched my family, friends, and neighbors buy not only guns but also a political philosophy of gun ownership. Decades before Michael Moore's *Bowling for Columbine* or the 9/11 terrorist attack on the World Trade Center, many in my community, along with millions of gun owners, have embraced a way of thinking about themselves and their country that has affected how they vote and how they think about freedom, crime, and the American way.

Ten years ago, at a gun show in Moscow, Idaho, I began to try to understand how and why guns speak in this national conversation. The men standing behind their folding tables selling an assortment of rifles, handguns, and ammunition lectured me on individual liberty, talking politics while they sold. They preached a brand of rugged individualism and exchanged stories about frontier heroes and combat missions in Vietnam and Korea.

This book follows that gun talk from gun shows, to gun stores, to gun-rights conventions, to the huge annual meetings of the National Rifle Association. I traveled to eight states, talking with gun owners, sellers, lobbyists, grassroots organizers, and policy makers. Some of these people are my neighbors, others I met far from home on the streets of Reno and Pittsburgh, at a county fairgrounds in Kankakee, Illinois, and on an Indian reservation in Worley, Idaho.

The journey I took to listen to this politics of guns made me question how we imagine what it means to be an American, and the often bitter debates that swirl around our identities as a people. Many of the stories I was told were about our revolutionary past and the American frontier. They were foundational beliefs for many Americans about how and why our nation was created, how the West was won, and even how we are a Christian nation and must fulfill a sacred, global destiny. And it was back to some of those tenacious stories about our past that I returned as I wrote this book. To understand gun talk, I had to understand what America means to millions of ordinary people and how these beliefs shaped their sense of who they are, were, and must remain in the future.

After all the miles I traveled and stories I heard, what this book made me see was how important gun politics were to white men. They were the main participants at the meetings and gun shows I attended. Gender and race informed most conversations I had. Even if white men promoted gun ownership as a necessary right of every American, the reasons for gun ownership depended upon an often highly racial and gendered view of America's history. And our popular culture has only reinforced this sense of how white men hold the destiny of the nation in their hands, especially if one hand holds a gun. For almost 150 years, Americans have watched as white men shot their way across our cinema screens, TV sets, Wild West shows, and theatre stages, making the world, and our cities and towns, safe from the bad guys. Guns often are equated with male action. And white men get to act more than anyone else in our popular imaginations, defending our freedoms and making the world safe for democracy.

I don't mean that women and people of color are not part of the story of guns in the United States. They were and still are. Especially today, women are encouraged to become shooters on screen and off. At gun shows, they are told that they need to practice self-defense and become armed citizens. In fact, entering the male world of guns is described as liberating, even empowering.[2] In this respect, the gun culture has not changed much since the 1880s, when women's shooting clubs were in vogue and white women who could afford the expense of a handgun or rifle were encouraged to know how to shoot and defend themselves against real and imagined enemies. Moreover, the arming and disarming of peoples of color has a long and traumatic history in the United States that exposes how ineffective we have been at providing basic security for all our citizens.

But most of the talk was with white men about white men.[3] Always the talk was about who had the right to own a gun and why, how this power was equated with individual freedom in the United States, and how without gun rights, as a people, we would slide into either anarchy or despotism. Guns were the safeguards of democracy.

As a white woman on this journey into gun talk, I did have two advantages. One, I was white, and two, I knew the fundamentals of shooting. I couldn't be labeled quickly as an ignorant liberal. Even though I am only a casual shooter, plinking at circular metal plates that spin, many women I know, including my daughter, will not touch a gun. Guns are bad, period. At gun shows, I am encouraged to touch guns. And the key word here is *touch*. The men selling know that women must cross a line to enter into the world of the gun, a line often equated not only with male action but also with male violence and the power of violence itself. And this appeal can be seductive for some women, even those who have no need for self-defense. But for many women I know, the widespread ownership of guns by men in the United States sets off angry red flares, the gun itself standing for all that is wrong with this country.

At one talk I gave in the Midwest, a young woman came up to me afterward and said she was no liberal gun-grabber. She didn't want to get close enough to grab a gun. She wanted men with guns to mind their own business and stay away from her. Period. Gun ownership was not an initiation into an American identity, nor was it a way to understand the rights and responsibilities of citizenship. Gun owners were gun nuts, crazies, and dangerous predators, particularly dangerous to women. The great

gun divide between men and women is reinforced by sheer statistics. According to the 1999 National Gun Policy Survey, only
12 percent of women own a gun while 44 percent of men do.[4]

Gun talk feeds and fuels the debates over individual rights
and how these rights rest on owning lethal force for political or
personal protection. In the gun-rights world, our personal liberties are defended by the use of lethal force in the hands of civilians, not in the hands of the state. Gun ownership is part and
parcel of democratic citizenship. In fact, a gauge of freedom is
determined by how much lethal force the government leaves in
the hands of individual citizens. The civil structures of government, with its checks and balances, its electoral processes, and
its social, economic, and military policies, only stand if individuals retain their weapons. Guns guarantee democracy.

The aisles of gun shows echo with these debates, and these
conversations can help us to understand why and how guns
hold such imaginative force for many Americans. It is important
to remember that gun shows are also traveling bookstores, gatherings for grassroots politics, and memory fairs of American history. They harbor small-scale and big-business entrepreneurs
across the aisle from mom-and-pop gun sellers who sell dreams
and a vision of the United States. Guns shows create imagined
communities, shaping what it means to be an American citizen.[5]

In the last twenty years, gun shows have also made some
Americans millionaires, and anyone with even the most cursory
knowledge of the arms industry knows what immense monetary
stakes are involved in gun sales to private individuals in the
United States. We have the largest domestic gun market in the
world. Since 1899, United States citizens have bought about
225 million firearms with approximately 192 million guns remaining in private possession.[6] Gun politics live and breathe in
the pages of gun magazines whose sole purpose is to sell a prod-

uct that comes complete with a way of life and a set of political beliefs. Guns circulate ideas and cash.

The freedom to buy is often equated with the right to keep and bear arms. At gun shows, the question about how much lethal power we can entrust to an individual is often answered with the response: as much as a gun owner wants. If a gun owner who is a law-abiding citizen wants a particular gun that is on the market, no questions should be asked. Regulation of individual buying behavior is a no-no, an infringement of rights guaranteed by the Constitution. Gun politics bring us into the world of male consumerism with its need to own the latest, the newest, and the most lethal gun there is. As a shooter, I have succumbed to this hype, lingering over ads for a few weeks of a new model .40 Sig Sauer that was adopted by the Air Marshals after 9/11. Gun manufacturers keep making new models to entice people to buy. And if the manufacturer can make it more lethal or look more lethal, so much the better for the ad campaign. In the 1840s, Samuel Colt developed this style of selling guns by continually making new models, what William Hosley has described as cannibalizing guns into different models to beat competitors.[7] Even at the annual meetings of the National Rifle Association, the big draw is the massive gun show at its heart, where the latest styles and accessories can be found. Hawking shiny gun hardware comes with the politics. Guns are cool things to buy, despite all the talk of rights and responsibility.

The American imagination has been held captive by the gun since before the Civil War, when gun markets of any consequence started in the United States.[8] Stories and pageants about the Western frontier became an early political theater for the staging of national dramas about heroes and their guns. My journey more than 150 years later into gun politics in the twenty-first century is inseparable from that early entertaining tale. As

Americans, we buy into and believe stories about our past that guide our values and our purchases.

The gun does indeed revolve in the American soul. But at what price? What alternative ways of imagining our democracy are never heard because the gun sounds so loud and true? Can we invent our lives without the noise of advertisers, gun-filled action movies, sound bites, and the constant pumping of anxiety through our national veins, making the gun the only safe harbor?

I believe we can. But not without first understanding how and why millions of Americans believe in the way of the gun.

GUN SHOW NATION

PART ONE

1

BUFFALO BILL AT THE GUN SHOW

M iles of graffiti-painted railroad cars with dancing pink, green, and white block letters were lugged past my car. Driving to a Peoria, Illinois, gun show, I had to hazard the inevitable train crossings, the minutes spent counting the cars or fussing over how late I would arrive. Massive black containers clanged past, and I tried to imagine the railroads that made Peoria a hub decades ago. The Rock Island Railroad used to stop here, and passengers could ride the *Rocket* to Chicago, singing the lyrics of a popular song praising the train, "Now listen to the jingle, and the rumble, and the roar, as she dashes thro' the woodland, and speeds along the shore."[1]

These railroads transformed prairies into a web of cities, connecting agricultural centers to capital markets, determining where people could build towns, start businesses, and live. The

Rock Island was a bonanza for a group of businessmen who wanted to connect Chicago with the Mississippi and get in on the ground floor of the economic boom in the Midwest. In the age of the great railroad barons like the Vanderbilts, Huntingtons, and Goulds, men made fortunes with the help of government subsidies, including the Homestead Act of 1862, which gave the railroads property rights to enormous tracts of public land. The scraps from the table went to the individual settlers. Peoria's economic health would rise and fall to the sound of the rails, and the city staggered when the rails went cold.[2]

This history of how corporations and capital settled the Midwest and West has always bored American audiences, who prefer to cheer instead for rugged Western heroes who blazed their way across the prairie and plains. For more than a century, a hard and fast belief in individual action, especially the quick-thinking determinism of frontier heroes, has captured the imagination of Americans.[3] I shouldn't have been surprised as I walked into the gun show at the Peoria Expo Gardens to find that in the heartland of Illinois the fantasy of the Wild West was alive and kicking.

As I walked past the guard at the front door and paid my entrance fee, I noticed a number of folding tables covered with Western guns. Gradually, I made my way over to a display with rifles and heard a guy in a black cowboy hat shout out, "This is more like it. Guns." He went on to complain to the man selling the rifles that he wondered if it was because the "ladies" were managing the show that it had gone soft. Not enough guns. He was pissed.

When I had first walked into the hall, I had seen out of the corner of my eye that there were a few coin exhibitors, and I'd been startled by the connection between coin and gun collecting. Later that day I talked with a woman selling coins who told me she had been coming to the show for thirty years. She explained that many gun shows wouldn't let in coin dealers. Their presence took away from the aura of the show. Guns, after all, weren't only collectibles: that would demean them into the oddball world of stamp, coin, and even beanie-baby geeks. The Peoria show also included a white woman selling 1920s racist kitsch: a large ceramic Mammy, books like *Little Black Sambo*, and ragstyle Melindy dolls.

Posters of Wild West shows were on sale at a nearby booth, along with buckles, pins, and jewelry—especially nineteenth-century scrimshaw. A sentimental image of a young girl with two twisted trees behind her was etched in black ink on a deep-ivory pin. Next to it lay a diminutive Smith & Wesson revolver, fit for a lady's hand. Pictures of Buffalo Bill Cody, the greatest Wild West showman, were also on display. And the prices were high. Not far away, a group of men huddled around a dealer in frontier firearms. He had a brown bearskin laid out across two tables and Winchester lever-action rifles on display. I hung around his tables and heard his complaints about the rich guys in St. Louis who spent up to $40,000 on vintage Western guns, the guys "who don't know what to do with money." He helped buyers locate specific rare guns and, like other dealers at the show, promoted the Wild West mystique to his customers.

Some of the goods at these booths were advertised as perfect for the Single Action Shooting Society (SASS) or Cowboy Action Shooting (CAS), recreation with period costumes that can set a shooter back thousands of dollars. Abigail A. Kohn has written about how the world of cowboy shooting romanticized the frontier and promoted values such as self-reliance, equality, and clear moral codes. Cowboy shooters believed in a mythic history that celebrated the conquest of the American frontier and valued an American national identity that found rejuvenation in the practice of violence.[4] And the guns marketed for cowboy and single-action shooting weren't cheap. Gun manufacturers recognized a good thing when it happened and had produced a new line of single-shot revolvers for cowboy shooters, such as the Ruger Bisley Vaquero, the Beretta Stampede, and replicas of the 1873 Colt "Peacemaker" and Winchester lever-action rifle. Through Umberti Arms, a wannabe cowboy could buy a piece of the Wild West in actual size for around $450, or, if he liked, in miniature for the same price.

The SASS booths at gun shows were usually located at the outer rim of exhibitors and staffed by enthusiastic men and women. When they found out I rode horses, they really pushed cowboy shooting. Entire magazines, newspapers, and specialty catalogs cater to the cowboy shooter, with dress-up outfits for gunslingers, lawmen, saloon girls, and Victorian ladies. There was a real dearth of cowboy shooters who could shoot from a horse. But then again, I didn't know many horses that liked to have guns fired while they were ridden. Even when the local cops would shoot in a meadow far from a barn where I kept my horse, the herds would go crazy. Hours of training were needed to reassure a horse—if it even has the temperament to tolerate the noise. Unless you hunted regularly on horses, had an old police horse, or were just plain committed to this shooting sport, it was hard to find good mounted cowboy shooters. It was easier to find the costumes, the jewelry, and the guns.

At another booth, I found a stack of books on the Wild West and purchased a 1911 second edition of *Thrilling Lives of Buffalo Bill, Colonel Wm. F. Cody, Last of the Great Scouts and Pawnee Bill, Major Gordon W. Lillie (Pawnee Bill) White Chief of the Pawnees* by Frank Winch.[5] Among the pages were a 1920s postcard of Buffalo Bill's grave on Lookout Mountain in Colorado, which I remembered visiting when I was young, and a photograph of Buffalo Bill with Theodore Roosevelt. Buffalo Bill, more than any other individual, made the western United States into a party, a play, a spectacle, and a product.[6] Coming of age as a pop icon at the same time that the railroad boom was happening, Buffalo Bill was the type of white male hero that fit the requirements the nation wanted at the end of the nineteenth century. Transported on railroad cars to more than 130 American cities each year, the shows helped Americans forget about the miles of rail and to imagine a landscape without industry, a place of buffalo hunts, heroes, and adventures. He was the ultimate man of action in a time when the little guy was being given smaller and smaller scraps from the national table. And he was clear about whom he hated and why.

Cody's 1879 autobiography, *The Life of Hon. William F. Cody, Known as Buffalo Bill,* captures the strain of a society emerging from civil war into a period of rapid economic and social change. Buffalo Bill began his life story by stressing the violence of pre–Civil War Kansas that almost destroyed his family. He wrote about how his father negotiated the explosive issue of slavery, by insisting that Kansas outlaw slavery and become a *"white* state" where "negroes, whether free or slave, should never be allowed to locate."[7] For that speech, his father was stabbed twice with a Bowie knife by a man who wanted slavery a guaranteed right in Kansas.

Cody survived the flames of Kansas, only to take his war to the plains, where he became an Indian killer and the ultimate promoter of himself as the frontier action hero. Fighting and killing Indians was more romantic than whites killing whites over slavery. And the frontier was imaginative miles away from the network of railroads choking the old frontier of the Midwest.

Of course, Cody had help becoming a star. For fourteen years before his Wild West Shows began in 1883, through stage plays, short stories, and novels, Buffalo Bill was invented, promoted, and adapted to the sensational mass markets of the time. In 1872, he performed in Ned Buntline's drama, *The Scouts of the Prairie*. For more than a decade, he or his clones patented a style of masculinity that was mimicked in life by men such as George Armstrong Custer. In 1876, when Buffalo Bill rejoined the army and took his first scalp for the defeated Custer, a scalp supposedly belonging to Chief Yellow Hand of the Cheyennes, he was immortalized even more certainly in the literary and stage mass markets. Cody had actually killed and scalped Yellow Hair, son of a Cheyenne chief named Cut Nose. But Yellow Hair was quickly elevated to chief for dramatic effect in Cody's retelling of the event and in the theatrical production *The Red Right Hand; or Buffalo Bill's First Scalp for Custer*. And Cody's revenge for the death of Custer made exciting stage drama and newspaper coverage in 1876, the year of the American centennial.[8]

Cody was also admired by Theodore Roosevelt, who promoted his own Western hero, the Anglo-American cowboy, in *Ranch Life and the Hunting-Trail* and later in *Winning of the West*. And in 1898, when Roosevelt put together his Rough Riders to fight Spain in Cuba, he enlisted cowboys and Indians along with wealthy, educated athletes and blue-blooded sportsmen. Roosevelt also offered up his cowboys to put down the labor strikes in Chicago that were threatening to put the brakes on the activities of the leaders of industry. [9]

That the action hero played as cowboy, scout, or Rough Rider lived on at the gun show was no surprise. Gun shows keep alive a mythic cultural past of the frontier that was started in the aftermath of the Civil War and then sustained for more than a hundred years by the genre of the Western in novels, dramas, rodeos, movies, television, popular music, and video games.

From 1860 to 1900, sensational fiction created thrills for the reader through the mass-produced, invented lives of white, male heroes. In the 1870s, dime novels were mass-produced in fiction factories, offering adventure stories for the working and middle classes. Buffalo Bill's character was a product of that book market. His adventures were cheaply reproduced in endless episodes and advertised for sale using the burgeoning techniques of marketing.

The Civil War had been hard on any sense of national unity among white men. More than 600,000 men had died and another 475,000 had been wounded, amputees often returning home to destroyed lives. Buffalo Bill restored this fragmented white hero through advertising, mass production, and sales, sales, sales.[10] He also provided a template for the emerging corporate and patriotic man: his autobiography depicted him leading buffalo hunts with newspaper moguls like James Gordon Bennett of the *New York Herald*, General Anson Stager of the Western Union Telegraph (one of the first monopolies in the United States), and several generals, majors, and colonels of the army, including General Philip Sheridan. Arriving on a special railroad car, the dignitaries played cowboys while Buffalo Bill dressed up in a manner that would render him a real man— and a man dressed for the occasion. From the clothing rack of American props culled from the violence of wars in the Southwest and West, he grabbed buckskin, sombrero, and crimson cowboy shirt to entertain the rich boys. He mounted a white horse and rode to camp with his rifle in his hand. He acted the part perfectly for his clients, who paid for the show. All the guests were eager to shoot buffalo, and one wanted to pretend the buffaloes were substitute Indians that he could shoot as fair game. The hunt ended in an extravagant feast of buffalo tail, prairie dog, rabbit, elk, antelope, black-tailed deer, wild turkey, teal, and mallard, and plenty of liquor: champagne, claret, whiskey, brandy, and ale.

While fiction factories may have produced Buffalo Bill, other factories were busy producing firearms to complete the fantasy. In 1873, the year after Buntline's *The Scouts of the Prairies* opened in Chicago, Colt Firearms was pushing its 1873 Peacemaker revolver and Winchester Repeating Arms Company was cranking out its Model 1873 Lever Action Rifle along with 250,000 cartridges of ammunition every day. At his death in 1862, Colt left behind an arms empire complete with a brilliant strategy to market his products. William Hosley writes about how Colt developed the art of advertising with paid testimonials from all the heroes he could find who would promote his guns.[11] He particularly liked testimonials from the combat field, and he entered into commissions with artist-adventurers such as George Catlin to market prints depicting Catlin's adventures, during which he'd used Colt products. Colt was a master at presentation pistols, and he greased the wheels of government contracts with many gold-engraved revolvers.

Like Buffalo Bill, Colt was a great self-promoter and enlisted the aid of celebrities whenever he could. He worked hard for government military contracts on both sides of the Atlantic— so hard that he was investigated for fraud and bribery—but he also understood that wars end and peace could be hard on the arms business. As Hosley points out, before characters like Buffalo Bill emerged in the mass market, the Texas Rangers were the "poster child of the New West."[12] Initially organized by the Texas Republic to protect Anglo settlers, they emerged as frontier heroes during conflicts in the 1840s with the Mexican army, Mexican guerrillas, and Indian tribes, hunting and killing Mexicans and Indians across the border and working for the interests of Anglo Texas ranchers.[13] Their testimonials advertised products with decorative frontier or combat scenes, machine-pressed into gun cylinders. These firearms at once told a story about nation building in the West and affirmed white manhood—an advertising formula that made Colt a bundle.

And the money was made through an industrial empire, where guns were produced by enforcing strict military discipline in factories. Some accounts say Samuel Colt demanded the silence of Sing Sing from his workers, often recent German immigrants who had been recruited for their talents as machinists and skilled mechanics. Gone were the quaint small-scale schemes of American capitalists, who looked with horror at the degraded wage slaves of the British factories. For the next fifty years, the United States rushed to build ever-larger factories with workers drawn from the countryside and throughout eastern and southern Europe, whose lives were regulated by the clock and whose resistance to their working conditions would create a violent struggle within the industry. Mass-produced from the factories of Winchester and Colt, guns were part of an immense shift in power that solidified corporate wealth and eventually built a nation that outstripped all others in arms manufacturing.[14]

Despite labor conflict, Colt's mini-machines, like sewing machines, railway engines, and printing presses, were industrial and technological wonders, gawked at by the masses and displayed with other amazing American products like the McCormick reaper at London's Crystal Palace in 1851, or the Corliss steam engines at the 1876 Philadelphia Centennial Exposition. At the 1893 World's Columbian Exposition in Chicago, gawkers could hoot at Buffalo Bill in his Wild West Show, gaze at the latest in gun manufacturing, and pretend that the labor violence and severe economic depression enveloping the city would soon go away.[15]

The Winchester Repeating Arms Company used Buffalo Bill's name whenever it could. The Wild West shows were a marketer's dream. Essential props in Buffalo Bill's Wild West Show included the Winchester Ammo Wagon and the many Winchester rifles used by Buffalo Bill in his scenes depicting Custer's Last Stand and his own revenge against Yellow Hair. Scenes inspired by the shows, such as buffalo hunts and Indian chases, were engraved on special rifles.[16] In fact, Winchester's own version of its corporate history credits Buffalo Bill with helping to sell its products, even though they never officially employed him.[17] The relationship between Buffalo Bill and Winchester was so close that even today the Buffalo Bill Historical Center in Cody, Wyoming, houses in its Cody Firearms Museum an extensive Winchester collection and describes their museum as the "most comprehensive assemblage of American firearms in the world."[18]

That these products and their celebrity counterparts still live on at the gun show in Peoria attests to their cultural and commercial power. The novelist of the old and new West, Larry McMurtry, has labeled Buffalo Bill and Annie Oakley the "first American superstars."[19] As celebrities, their showmanship with rifles made guns into icons for the masses. Buying the guns of the frontier meant the possession of a piece of the nation's mythic history and power, like a relic of a saint's hair or bone.

As I walked the aisles looking at the single-shot revolvers, I recalled that one of the guns I used to shoot periodically was a Sturm, Ruger Single-Six, a 1953 clone of Colt's 1873 "Peacemaker," a fantasy gun, what some observers of modern society would call a fetish, a gun saturated in meanings.[20] The mystique of the Western gun rested on an inflated belief in the individual and the power within the reach of an ordinary human being.

The male clone, whether he was Buffalo Bill, Tom Mix, or John Wayne, always got his man, always triumphed, always ended the hero. Like the romance novel for women, which promised and delivered love and money in fictional form, the gun in fiction and in reality convinced and reassured men that personal power was only a trigger-pull away. In the late nineteenth century, the gun protected its owner from the realities of power in a highly competitive world, just like romance novels protected women from the harsh world of nagging doubt, loneliness, and economic want.[21] It was a trade-off, a modern exchange. The harsh and often violent conflicts of industrial capitalism, the brutal tactics of political repression, and the racial hatreds inherent in American expansionism at the turn of the century faded as Buffalo Bill rode the rails, bringing the Wild West show and its guns to millions of Americans.

My 1953 clone of a single action revolver was only one piece of a booming cultural industry of Westerns, Western wear, and frontier guns in the United States after World War II. In the shadow of a nuclear arms race and the sudden and permanent irrationalities of thermonuclear war, a new set of cowboys entered radio, TV, movies, and rodeos to entertain and once again value particular behaviors in men. Keeping in step, the six-shooter line revved up for another peak in sales. Companies like Sturm, Ruger and Colt met the demand by reproducing 1873 Colt models and a factory line of other frontier guns.

From the 1850s to today, Colt industries and many arms manufacturers like Winchester have not been so different from fashion designers who repackage, rename, and refit their models to create new product lines. A great challenge to Colt was to make the gun—a weapon designed to kill—a morally acceptable product. Armed individuals can wreak havoc in any nation, rioting, fermenting labor strikes, separating into violent factions, and even splitting into warring camps. The Civil War showed how deadly the game of nation building could become.[22]

To make the gun morally acceptable, Colt Firearms and the massive arms industry that followed to supply the domestic market needed to make the gun owner a simple moral hero who killed without nagging doubts and with the stamp of national approval. Dressed in a white hat and mounted on a white horse, he never hesitated in his call to duty. Enter the Buffalo Bills of the world, whose packaged morality created a checklist of enemies who could be shot with impunity.

Buffalo Bill's autobiography validated a cult of death that served nation-building goals, the conquest and clearing of Western lands, the unquestioned acceptance of corporate growth, and simplified gender and race roles. In its pages, Cody slaughtered hundreds of buffalo and dozens of Indians, and he laughed through the carnage. He made the violence of the frontier acceptable, and he made the savagery of the railroad barons disappear. His state-sanctioned masculinity was a necessary social glue for a world connecting immense capital with the seizure of indigenous lands. He was the wild. He was death. He was the ultimate con artist who could sell, sell, and sell.

At Peoria's gun show, the glow of the Western hero kept alive a low-rent version of this male consumer history. At many of the gun shows I attended, the frontier hero and his guns had been pushed aside by a new line of high-tech gun products and male clones, warrior guys like Arnold and Sylvester and video-game heroes, packing military weapons, knocked off in sport and domestic models. Western firearms were still showcased at special gun shows in cities like Dallas, Albuquerque, and Reno, but Western heroes lived on more through a style of masculinity than an abundance of new six-shooters for sale.

Instead, what I saw in Peoria was the persistence of a 150-year-old cultural fantasy that continued to feed a potent form of national identity politics. Buffalo Bill made gun ownership moral, fun, and normative in the emotional landscape of white manhood. With the gun, the individual man could walk, talk, and live like a hero. His national identity reassured, he could forget how his ordinary life was dependent upon and often trapped within an economic and social system not of his making, in which his value was counted out in minutes, hours, and days.

Walking out of the gun show, I passed by a pickup truck with a MY PRESIDENT IS CHARLTON HESTON bumper sticker. How fitting. The past president of the National Rifle Association was a showman, a product promoter, and an action hero. In 1953, Charlton Heston even played Buffalo Bill in *Pony Express*. The latest incarnation of a series of male replicants, Heston helped Americans imagine their world once again through the lens of nostalgia and purchases. And in 2003, Heston was rewarded with the Presidential Medal of Freedom for his commitment to the nation. Samuel Colt and Buffalo Bill would have been proud.

2

REBIRTH OF A NATION

In the spring of 2002, I attended an NRA committee meeting on the media and listened to Armstrong Williams, a conservative African American TV, radio, and newspaper columnist, talk about how he grew up in South Carolina and hunted deer, raccoon, and quail. The people he knew were responsible with guns; there were no accidental shootings. After he moved to Washington, D.C., he paid attention when his mother asked him: "Boy, do you have a gun in this house?"

She strongly recommended a shotgun; he agreed, and he drove to Virginia to buy one. Williams reminded the audience that there were people in the world who were "ruthless." "It's a matter of life and death," he said. He watched forensic television shows and tried to see inside the criminal mind. He urged everyone in the audience to protect themselves and their families. His periodic words of encouragement were unequivocal: "Arm yourselves." "Be proud when you bear that arm." "There is nothing wrong in killing for self-defense. I'd rather they died, than you died." His voice struck out loud and clear with a Pentecostal urgency. And his white audience sat nodding their heads.

The group had come to hear about the media and really did not need Williams to convince them that guns were necessary for personal self-defense. But the fact that an African American man was doing the talking, a man who agreed with their politics and joined in the liberal-bashing by the other panelists, made the moment sweet for the neoconservatives and libertarians in the room. Williams was making a simple equation for the audience. "Black" did not mean "liberal." His presence was no obstacle to the tirades on the panel against liberals taking over the media, even when one panelist insisted that liberals were "not stupid": they were "evil." He said nothing when one audience member urged everyone in the room not to make friends with liberals. Even if they felt tempted, they must resist. "They absolutely believe they are better than us."

Williams's defense of guns to fight criminals rang with irony. African Americans have been organizing, petitioning, and pursuing every political and legal option they have had for more than two hundred years to find protection through effective civil government. Guns have been the last line of defense when government broke down under the weight of racism and economic opportunism. Left largely without civil, political, or police protection from the writing of the United States Constitution and the Bill of Rights until well into the twentieth century, free blacks, slaves, and then black citizens have often had to rely on themselves and their communities to survive. Their armed self-defense has had a troubled political history as the law, public opinion, and mass culture in the North and South have upheld the disarming of black Americans for that same two hundred years.

Before the Civil War, slaves were severely restricted from owning or carrying firearms unless they were hunting on their plantations or acting under orders from their masters, often to serve in armed units to fight indigenous tribes. Freed blacks in both the North and South faced discrimination when they attempted to join militia and military units to act in defense of their country, even though they were periodically called upon to fight. And they faced additional barriers when they attempted to purchase guns to defend themselves against federal-, state-, and county-sanctioned violence against their persons, families, and property.[1]

At the same time that Buffalo Bill walked the boards in his exciting adventures, puffing up white heroes with guns in the 1870s, whites in the post-Reconstruction South were engaged in violence against blacks that would result in their loss of one of the basic principles of government—to provide security for its citizens. By 1877, Reconstruction had stopped and with it the federal and popular will to sustain political change in the Southern states. Republicans, as the party of Lincoln, would go down in defeat throughout the South, and Democrats would taste victory as they pursued a policy of restricting and even abolishing the political and legal rights of freed slaves. Worse, targeted violence by whites against blacks would create a sense of siege for many black Southerners.[2] Despite the Fifteenth Amendment to the Constitution, written after the Civil War to protect the vote for freed slaves, by the 1930s, almost no blacks voted in the Southern states.[3] Each state constitution had amended its requirements for voting to stop such challenges to white rule. Elaborate but effective statutes and laws closed the polls for millions of Southern citizens. Not until the Voting Rights Act of 1965 would Southern blacks begin again the long process of voter registration and access to government necessary for political representation and protection.

The ballot and the gun have a close, disturbing history for African Americans. The effective disarmament of blacks was necessary to create an apartheid regime in the Southern states. Alongside the restrictions on firearms were the laws against owning land and voting. One of the landmark Supreme Court cases that addressed the right to bear arms happened during the Reconstruction while federal troops were still in the Southern states to bolster the democratically elected state governments who were increasingly besieged by armed white supremacists.[4] The gun violence that brought the case to the Court was directly related to the ballot.

Recently, Robert M. Goldman has investigated what history has called the Colfax Massacre.[5] He described how William Ward, a black Union Army veteran, was "appointed by Governor Warmoth to lead and train the local militia in Grant parish," named after U. S. Grant, the president of the United States.[6] His eventually all-black militia company fought with arms against the relentless violence of the Ku Klux Klan. This armed black man was a seasoned veteran, fighting for his civil rights. He armed to protect himself, his family, his community, and his rights to vote and own land. He was legally authorized by the governor as a member of a local militia to protect these political rights because many whites in Louisiana had no intention to protect them at all.

After the Louisiana elections of 1872, Grant parish descended into violence to resolve their political differences.[7] At the end of the elections, both Fusionists (a mix of Northern carpetbaggers and Democrats) and the opposing Republicans claimed victory at the polls. When the governor declared the Republican sheriff and judge victors in Grant parish, William Ward, with a group of black men and the newly elected sheriff and judge, opened a window of the Colfax courthouse and climbed in, claiming what they felt was legally theirs.

What followed was another chapter in the stripping of political rights from black citizens in the final years of Reconstruction. Negotiations broke down between the gathering whites that surrounded the courthouse and the anxious blacks that had fled there for protection. Soon, three hundred armed white men began to exchange fire with the men inside the courthouse. Two whites were shot; we probably will never know by whom. Then the slaughter began. People fleeing the building were shot down. Some of their bodies were mutilated and thrown into the Red River; others were left where they dropped. About fifty people were taken prisoner and shot later, execution-style. One elderly black man, Benjamin Brimm, although shot through the head and back, survived to become a key witness before a federal grand jury. In the end, no one was convicted for the killings.

Easter Sunday, 1873, in Colfax, Louisiana would prove once and for all that African Americans could not defend with arms either their lives or their right to vote even if they were members of a local militia. Under siege, they had no protection at either the state or national level. Whites in the South and North were turning their backs on the political, economic, and personal security of black citizens. In 1875, after repeated delays, the Supreme Court in *United States v. Cruikshank* unanimously decided that the indictments against the accused murderers were faulty. The federal acts written in 1870 to enforce freedoms for blacks would prove vague and ambiguous under the scrutiny of federal judges eager to return the task of law enforcement to the Southern states.

The judicial shell game of post–Civil War America had begun. Blacks pleaded for justice and found none in either the state or federal courts. The Fourteenth Amendment that tried to defy the state's abuse of power was gutted and what Mark Twain had called "The United States of Lyncherdom" reared its ugly head.[8] Abandoned to the amended constitutions of the Southern states, black citizens gradually lost most political rights. It would be a long ninety years until the Voting Rights Act of 1965, and even longer before Louisiana began to protect its black citizens.

Gun-control advocates point to the 1875 Supreme Court decision to prove that the Second Amendment does not guarantee an individual the right to own a gun. Gun lobbyists for individual rights argue that the 1875 decision was a travesty. In their recent interest in nineteenth-century history, they use the disarming of freed blacks through the Black Codes and state constitutions to underscore a passionate need to guarantee the individual a constitutional right to own a gun.

I can't but wonder whether, if William Ward were alive today, he would cringe at this loss of memory. During the fighting at the Colfax Courthouse, he saw the imminent danger to his fellow militiamen and his neighbors, who, without the legal protections of government, were targets for those who took the law into their hands with impunity. The fight to the death was over the courthouse. In the midst of the chaos, Ward was able to leave the besieged building and travel to New Orleans in search of federal aid. A fellow militiaman, Levin Allen, was left in charge. But relief came too late. No federal troops swept down on the courthouse to stop the violence. Federal troops, who arrived the day after the shooting stopped, instead counted the bodies strewn along the roads, fallen in the woods, and floating in the river. They tried to follow the trail of the shooters. In the end only nine men were arrested and brought to trial.

The black militiamen at the Colfax courthouse fought for their lives, but they also fought for their right to have government. They fought against hostile, armed neighbors unwilling to accept their rights as common citizens. They fought with the newly elected sheriff and judge by their side. They fought as individuals and as African Americans under siege in their own land. This connection is what is lost today. By making the gun debate rest on individual rights alone, we have torn the debate from the historical struggle of minorities and women to gain the protection of government. And we have forgotten how culturally important the disarming of blacks was to many white Americans.

Nowhere is this point better illustrated than in the first cinematic blockbuster in the United States, *The Birth of a Nation* by D. W. Griffith, released in 1915 with a personal showing at the White House to President Woodrow Wilson and his friends. After the Civil War, nostalgic stories about Southern plantation life joined with frontier tales to reimagine the past and reinvent the future of a nation. Memorializing not only the Civil War but also postwar elections in the South, the film depicted freed blacks as illiterate clowns and predatory thugs. Claiming the status of documentary truth for his scenes of "historical facsimile," Griffith used humor to depict black citizens abusing their newly won political power in the 1870 South Carolina House of Representatives, and he depicted sexual terror as the result of freed blacks wielding military power.

In Griffith's depiction of the Reconstruction South, black federal militiamen of the same status as William Ward walked the sidewalks of Piedmont, South Carolina, refusing to defer to traditional white power and privilege by not stepping off the sidewalks. These soldiers were ultimately disarmed in the film because they were represented as posing an emotional and sexual threat to the white women of the town, especially two daughters, one of a Southern planter and the other a Northern politician. In the finale, whites from North and South banded together to defeat the lascivious advances of Gus, a black captain in the militia, and Silas Lynch, a newly elected mulatto lieutenant governor. The horrid violence of the Civil War was transformed into a fraternal union of whites who restore political and military rule to the nation.

In *The Birth of a Nation*, scenes of attempted rape and sexual violence justify the disarming of blacks who were militia members and elected politicians. The armed and mounted Klu Klux Klan rose to defend the South in this filmic hysteria over the purity of white womanhood. The sexual myth promoted by Griffith buries the true history of the political struggles during Reconstruction. Freed blacks during Reconstruction were intent on gaining political and economic ground. They worked to legitimize their slave marriages, find economic and educational opportunities, and pursue political rights. Blacks who had fought in the Civil War for the Union forces and had returned after the war to serve in state and federal militia units were a threat to the reestablishment of white rule in Southern states. Their disarming was part of an overall political strategy to deny them votes, jobs, and land.[9]

The historian Otis A. Singletary wrote in the 1950s about the alarming levels of violence in the South after the Civil War, much of this violence directed against the "Negro militia movement."[10] In his study, he found that not only the Klan but also the political force of Southern conservatives challenged and redefined state militia laws to eliminate black militias. In this atmosphere, black militia captains were executed, arms were confiscated, and militiamen were attacked, pushed out of communities, or killed. Whites assisting or socializing with black militiamen also became targets of violence. Further, volunteer rifle companies, often made up of former Confederate soldiers, organized into groups like White Line, White League, People's Club, Red Shirts, and White Man Party to overturn by force both the black militias and the new Radical or Republican governments of the South.[11]

These volunteer rifle companies were "an aggressive political instrument welded into a military mold for a definite purpose."[12] Their well-armed officers had experience in Civil War combat; they operated in broad daylight and did not care about hiding under white hoods. The money for the club guns came from local and regional fund-raisers, but there was also evidence that funds for the rifles came from the Democratic organization "privately subscribed in the North."[13] Throughout the South, "race riots that took place between whites and the militia were deliberately planned."[14] President Grant tried to disband rifle companies in South Carolina, but they returned with social club names that parodied their own violent intent, calling themselves the First Baptist Church Sewing Circle or the Hampton and Tilden Musical Club.[15]

The cinematic violence of *The Birth of a Nation* replayed these historical armed confrontations. Contemporary reports indicate that theatre crowds went wild with applause when the Klan rode to the rescue of the fair white maidens and returned to town to confiscate the guns from the black militia. In the congressional reports of the 1870s on turmoil in the Southern states, supposedly used by Thomas Dixon to write *The Clansman*, which was later adapted by Griffith to create *The Birth of a Nation*, witnesses to the violence surrounding the political elections that year record how Klansmen intimidated black men and white women. Blacks were kept away from polls, and white women who served blacks in restaurants, taverns, or as prostitutes faced physical retaliation. Some women testified to a different form of sexual violence than Griffith's depictions: their pubic hair was burnt for associating with black men. Yet, this story would not have resolved for white audiences their anxieties about the political, economic, and social equality of the races. Only cultural hysteria over a white woman's rape would afford them justification for the continued repressive government of white rule.[16]

One of the many ironies of the movie is that Griffith needed so many mounted Klan horsemen to ride to the rescue of white women that he had to borrow cowboys from film sets where Westerns were being cranked out at the time. The plantation and the frontier played together for millions of Americans.

The Colfax Massacre and *The Birth of a Nation* illustrate the contradictions of gun culture. Listening to Armstrong Williams, I think about Gus in *The Birth of a Nation*. In Griffith's blockbuster, the black man becomes a predator and a criminal, unworthy of his rank as a captain in the militia. Discussion of politics and civil government disappears underneath the frenzy of attempted rape. Anxiety about the shifts in political and economic power are drowned out by the emotional rhetoric of crime.

Armstrong Williams can proclaim himself an arch-conservative, but he still is a strange bedfellow in gun culture. At most gun shows I attend, I am able to buy latter-day versions of *The Birth of a Nation*. Even at shows that are supposedly checked for Nazi and racist propaganda, I can pick up pamphlets, books, and newspapers that describe the twenty-first-century world of black criminals who kill, rob, and maim, and the violent juvenile predators that stalk Americans who have only the gun to defend themselves from the racial violence of black youth. I can buy the *Turner Diaries* and read about how black cops are going to break down my door and force their brutal rule on my lily-white soul.

The gun in America reeks of white power. Its history is inseparable from keeping arms in the hands of whites and disarming black men to prevent their access to political and economic power. It is part of a romantic tale of white frontier heroes and valiant Southern plantation owners rescuing their white daughters from the hands of black predators. With the imagined threat of black violence breathing down the backs of white Americans scampering to the suburbs and exburbs, gun culture has effectively funneled and fueled white anxieties.

Armstrong Williams and Roy Innis, the head of the Congress for Racial Equality (CORE), who was reelected to the NRA board in 2002 for another three-year term, both strongly promote an individual's right to own a gun. In recent years, the NRA has even described itself as "the oldest Civil Rights organization" because of this insistence on the right to self-defense with a gun. And in the midst of this fight over individual rights, the NRA has opposed the National Association for the Advancement of Colored People (NAACP), which actually *is* the oldest civil rights organization in the United States. In an attempt to curb access to guns in black urban neighborhoods, gun-control measures and the regulation of arms manufacturers, distributors, and dealers have been supported by such organizations as the NAACP and other black leaders.[17] These attempts have run up against the powerful political force of the NRA.

These tensions were highlighted in 2001 during the annual

Martin Luther King, Jr., dinner given by CORE.[18] Present to receive a humanitarian award was Reverend Leon Sullivan, the American civil rights leader who wrote the Sullivan Principles, which held corporations responsible to society and pushed for change in apartheid South Africa. According to several newspaper reports, Sullivan spoke passionately for wide-scale economic and political reform in the United States and the world. He called on African Americans to help Africans in their struggle against AIDS, unemployment, and gun violence. He challenged the gun lobby to get guns off the streets.

Charlton Heston, the president of the NRA, also spoke that night, saying, "All people have an inalienable right to defend their lives and their liberty from whoever would harm them and with whatever means necessary." In Heston's words, democratic political struggles became irrelevant to the protection of person and property. Government instead must function to uphold the inalienable right of individuals "to defend their lives and their liberty." And what's more, citizens were immune to regulation in choosing "whatever means necessary." Each individual—gun in hand—became an army of one left to defend home and liberty. Like in a science fiction movie, civil structures had ceased to advocate and promote change for economic and social justice. And the ballot was a crucial means to keep the gun in the hand. Though he spoke on the importance of the civil rights movement, Heston advocated a politics of individual gun ownership to cure America of its social ills.

William Ward, the black militiaman in the Colfax courthouse, would have been glad to know the positive effects of black voting rights after 1965 in the South. The historian Frank R. Parker traced an immediate decline in violence by whites when blacks voted and elected officials in Mississippi.[19] The right to government begins to ease the reign of terror that Southern blacks had experienced for almost one hundred years. William Ward's efforts must not be forgotten amidst the high-pitched rhetoric of gun rights. The armed citizen can in the end only protect as far as his gun can shoot. Government of the people and for the people can protect an entire land.

3

THE RIFLE FRATERNITY

The woods smelled of sweet grass, dank spruce, and thick fir. Driving along a narrow road to the rifle shooting range, I thought about the effort needed to even arrive at the point of shooting a rifle. Earlier in the day, cleaning gear was spread on newspapers across my dining room table. A bottle of Hoppe's #9 Solvent, white cotton squares, and a cleaning rod were used to make certain the oil that coated the metal, barrel, and bolt of the rifle while it was in storage was gone. Additional checks were made on sights, ammunition, earplugs, earmuffs, protective glasses, and a first-aid kit, just in case. The rituals of safety were methodically followed and would be repeated after the shooting was done to rid the barrel of the residue of firing, what is called "gunpowder fouling." "Good habits," is what my instructor said, "repeated again and again."

Unlike some shooting ranges I have visited that are thrown together in fields or at the edge of quarries, with rickety and rusty targets and trash bins loaded with beer cans, this range was picture-perfect, set in a knoll between sculptured hills, with clearly marked distances and sets of paper targets, though my instructor remarked that they were not as well aligned as they could be. The geometry and exact measurement of space and distance make rifle shooting into a sport dependent on optics, eyesight, and methodical practice. A park ranger had us register, pay the fee, and read the rules. One stood out: he could refuse or eject a shooter and command a cease-fire on the range. Protocols of shooting were strictly enforced.

When we arrived, an elderly man was on the range, hunched over a vintage Enfield rifle that he took care to clean on the range after he fired it. He didn't even wait for the drive home. Each crack from his gun hit the hills and resonated, expanding and deepening. His shooting pace was slow and deliberate, with minutes spent on adjusting sights, rearranging rifle rests, and positioning the body to take the best shot.

My instructor had first shot a rifle in Scouts, then later on the rifle team in college, and then much later hunting in South Dakota, Wisconsin, Colorado, and the Pacific Northwest. After losing the need or desire to hunt any longer, he was left again with the shooting range and paper targets. Handing me the rifle, he told me it was about the perfect score, controlling the breath, following through the squeeze of the trigger, and learning how not to flinch. The recoil and the noise of the rifle lead to anticipation and a nervous twitch that could ruin the shot. It was all about self-control, discipline, and the shedding of unwanted reflexes.

At the end of the nineteenth century, Arthur Corbin Gould, the editor of *The Rifle* magazine, and George Wingate, one of the founders of the National Rifle Association, would have heartily agreed, though they would have added that rifle discipline was an essential practice for the patriotic and militarily prepared white male citizen. A cultural push to transform white American men into riflemen came at a time when men of business and the professions needed to prove their grit, and state militias provided a means to advocate a strong national manhood. Like other European powers at the end of the century, the United States was pursing its own path to imperialism in the Caribbean and the Pacific. Not only military men, but also civilians who were prepared to pick up a rifle and fight with the moral mission of civilization and industry, were needed by the nation to serve on the battlefronts of Cuba and the Philippines.[1] By the 1890s and Wounded Knee, the conquest of Western lands and indigenous peoples was complete. The rifleman was the disciplined partner of Buffalo Bill's impulsive and archaic force.

Citizen soldiers trained as riflemen were hard to find at the end of the nineteenth century. State militias had become volunteer organizations, like fraternal clubs promoting all-male sports with civic pride.[2] They were the volunteer remnants of citizen-soldiers. Some of these state militia units had ties with an earlier period of communal and universal military duty under local command. But these old kinship and town militia units had morphed during the century into class-conscious and often ethnically exclusive social clubs with a studied military gloss.[3]

Periodically derided by the press and the regular military as tin or holiday soldiers, these volunteer citizen-soldiers appeared more decorative than combative as they paraded, marched, and dressed in spectacular uniforms. Many state militia units were constantly begging for state funds to provide even basic training for their members; others, such as the Eastern Seaboard units of New York and Massachusetts, had long histories and ample funding, sometimes provided through private balls and theatricals. Their officers were successful businessmen, even retired officers of the regular army, and they loved to sing the praises of the citizen-soldier even if the nation had rejected its reality long before.

With Gould and Wingate, certain key leaders in the state militias believed a constantly vigilant citizenry was needed to keep the nation safe and ready to fight. They were wary of immigrants and fearful that these men might not provide the right stuff for either the volunteer state militias or the regular military. They argued for the cultivation of a select group of expert white men to assist the militia as officers and even help train "raw recruits" for the regular military. As H. Richard Uviller and William G. Merkel have noted, the volunteer militia was often both selective and elite in its recruitment and membership, looking down on the "contemptible militia-of-the-whole."[4] The right men were needed as citizen-soldier riflemen, and they would provide an unofficial "reserve" force for the country.

Under Gould's management, *The Rifle* magazine lasted only three years. In 1888, it changed its name to *Shooting and Fishing,* complicating its advocacy of the rifle to include the turn-of-the-century craze for the "more innocent pleasures" of fly-fishing. And after the death of its editor, the magazine once again transformed, becoming between 1906 and 1923 *Arms and the Man,* a strong advocate of what was by then called the National Guard, during which time the NRA purchased the magazine, changing its name in 1924 to *The American Rifleman.* Even though *The American Rifleman* claimed that its precursor was started in 1885 under the name *The Rifle,* the National Rifle Association did not take over *Arms and the Man* until the disruptions of World War I, when the National Guard effectively came under federal control.

The glorification of riflemen in these early years tells much about the conflicts over male citizenship and masculinity in the United States. Coming from the professional and business classes, the officers of the state militias addressed multiple audiences: their fellow militia members, citizens, and the military. And they spoke with a patrician voice of morality that both selected and converted men to their vision of expert riflemen, unlike the undisciplined rabble whose weapons of choice might be cheap revolvers, dangerous pistols, knives, or razors and who might end up as "raw recruits" if war came. The training the officers of the state militias could provide would discipline both the mind and the body to produce both modern workers and adept soldiers when their country called.

Yet, instead of fighting in wars that expanded the national and imperial reach of the United States, citizen-soldiers in state militias were more frequently called upon to stop labor strikes and assist in natural disasters at home.[5] The industrial and capital expansion that fed imperialism also fueled massive labor unrest in railroad yards and factories during the 1870s and for decades afterward.[6] Volunteer state militias were often thrown into explosive domestic disturbances and sent to protect the property of corporations against railroad and mining strikers. Their responses in these conflicts were both praised and damned. State militiamen came under attack by the public, the press, and the federal army as ineffective and incompetent in arms, prejudiced against or sympathetic to workers, or even violent thugs for corporations. And the officers of the state militia were further criticized as ineffective wealthy businessmen and lawyers who had landed extra pay and fancy uniforms through corrupt patronage without a clue about how to lead men in battle.[7]

Under Gould's editorship, *The Rifle* magazine argued for systematic rifle training for the state militia. And he promoted the "noble sport" of rifle-shooting through civilian rifle clubs that could perfect the techniques of rifle practice, create a civilian reserve of trained riflemen that would volunteer in state militias and the regular army if they were needed for foreign wars, and offer a manly form of recreation for men of business, the professions, and skilled labor, particularly mechanics and machinists.[8] The pages of *The Rifle* praised the benefits of the rifle-shooting sports as good for competitive health, technical knowledge, self-control, and nervous disorders. Rifle practices, the suggestion was, train the right men for the modern demands of work with the added benefit of creating a reserve pool of patriotic civilians prepared for military service.

George W. Wingate also believed in the benefit of systematic and supervised rifle training. A successful New York lawyer and an officer in the state militia, he developed a system of rifle practice modeled on British techniques. Wingate envied the National Rifle Association of Great Britain and named his own New York rifle club after it, hoping to create a similar national organization. His group struggled, fighting regional tensions about sport-shooting rules, handicapping, and a lack of general interest in the sport. By 1892, the NRA was defunct, only to be reborn in 1896 in connection with the New Jersey state militia.

But the origins of Wingate's New York organization reveal much about the fears and desires of these early upper-class riflemen. Despite what the NRA might promote about the American past, Wingate believed that Americans were not a nation of riflemen. What he saw in the Civil War and in the streets of New York confirmed his beliefs that the way out of this moral and social dilemma was to promote a new type of white manhood, based on rifle practice. Only then could the sloppy, panic-stricken, or indifferent American white male finally measure up and become a man, ready to act as a proper soldier when called upon by his state or his country to aim true and fire. He also advocated for boyhood training through the schools and colleges and for consistent practice through civilian rifle clubs that competed with militiamen. Manhood and the future preparedness of the nation for war rested on this civilian training.

Why Wingate was so firm about his beliefs becomes clearer when we understand what was at stake. In New York, the so-called 1871 Orange Riots exploded on the streets of the city.[9] When a small group of Protestant Orangemen marched on July 12, 1871, despite intense fears among the city's police that Irish Catholics would attempt to stop them, police and state guard units were under order by New York Governor John T. Hoffman to protect the marchers along their route. With the violence of the draft riots during the Civil War fresh in their memory, the police and the guard units, which had grown to a troop strength of 5,327 men, escorted the Orangemen through the city streets. Stones were thrown, insults were leveled, and at a few intersections, shots were fired from both the crowd and buildings along the route.

In response, the militia fired into the crowd of both spectators and protesting Irish Catholics. Fifty-five of the sixty-two people who died that day were killed by militia fire, with about sixty of the 100 injuries also the result of militia fire. And witnesses reported that militia saluted and cheered their fellow Protestants and even provoked the violence in the streets. Irish newspapers attacked the use of the militia and struck out against its use to support business interests, punish Irish laborers and unions, and squelch the republican traditions of the

Irish people. The heat was high. And in this instance the militia rifle fired along class and ethnic lines. Renamed a "militia riot" by the historian Michael Gordon, the Orange Riots proved that the New York Guard would turn its rifles on citizens, firing into a crowd even without orders.

Russell S. Gilmore suggested in his study of American rifle games that this incident contributed to the creation of the National Rifle Association since Colonel Church and George Wood Wingate began the NRA two months after the Orange Riots to improve the marksmanship of the New York Guard.[10] Certainly, Wingate believed that the "results of this riot were to impress upon the leading officers of the National Guard the importance and, in fact, the necessity of instructing the different regiments in rifle practice."[11] And the riot further "helped the work of the National Rifle Association."[12] Wingate believed in the face of this complex city violence that what the militia needed primarily was better training in rifle practice to help create order. If properly trained with the rifle, the citizen-soldier in the militia would act properly. Further, civilians could play an essential part in this training by consistent competitive practice with militiamen on specially built rifle ranges. As part of his efforts, he oversaw the creation of the Creedmoor shooting range on Long Island at which both civilians and militia competed.

Many writers have pointed out the links between the National Rifle Association and its military past, but what is significant was how the civilian rifleman emerged in the pages of *The Rifle* as a type of American male that the country desperately needed while the United States was rocked with racial, ethnic, and labor violence and would soon be flexing its muscles in Cuba and the Philippines.[13] He was not the rowdy Irish laborer with a pistol hidden in his clothes or shooting from a tenement window, the dago with a knife, or the Negro with a razor. His profile, as featured in the pages of *The Rifle* and *Shooting and Fishing*, was that of a respected member of the community, a college boy, businessman, bookkeeper, skilled machinist, or lawyer, a man of means who would submit himself to the discipline of rifle practice and help lead the nation to future glory.

Wingate helped to create an ideal man through rifle training when rifles were diminishing in importance as part of modern warfare, replaced by machine guns, artillery fire, air power, and naval bombardment.[14] The point of Wingate's new improved rifle exercises was to train the mind and body of the shooter to fire with accuracy and composure under command and under fire. The development of competitive sport shooting often had little relevance to the battlefield.[15] Like the development of golf, rifle sport shooting for civilians appealed to a moneyed class of men who could afford the time, equipment, and travel to compete in serious games.[16]

As disciplined recreation, competitive rifle shooting encouraged habits that the business class liked. Applauded in the pages of these early magazines was off-hand shooting of the rifle with the shooter standing because it tested the nerves and strength, a style not encouraged in warfare, when the prone position with an attached sling or improvised rest is safer and more reliable. This ideal of the rifleman harbored a contradiction at its core. The rifleman had limited use as a practical model for the white civilian male ready to switch in an instant to military mode. Once a military man, the rifleman was quickly becoming a specialist in modern war, a sniper. His training in rifle practice was reduced in the military to specialized tactics in killing at long distances, or dull basic training in repetitive drill. More an extension of the rifle and a replaceable part, the military man who pulled the trigger was rewarded insofar as he aimed accurately and fired when told to fire. He did not run and he did not think. His enemy was constructed by the policies of his nation and reduced to a target.

When I asked men at my visits to gun shows what their gun would say if it could talk, they often don't carry on about who it wanted to shoot, but how it wanted to shoot with deadly aim. The rifle had no ethical voice. Gun talk was the whispered instructions in the mind, repeated to discipline the body to complement what the gun was designed to do. The pull of the finger on the trigger, the heft against the shoulder or in the hand, the stillness of the breath before fire, the mind emptied of all but focus on the immediate task. Since rifles were designed for shooting targets at distances, their skillful use continued to present tactical problems for the military and the state militia, and enormous social and political problems for local governments, who had to decide whether to use them at all on their streets—against their citizens, against newly arrived immigrants, or against angry strikers.

Competitive rifle shooting was also doomed in another way. According to Gilmore, the NRA died because the interest in long-range rifle marksmanship and training depended upon the continued interest of an upper social class and the existence of shooting ranges large enough to support the sport. With the rise in urban land values, the ranges closed, and the interest in rifle shooting declined, replaced by the trick shooting of Wild West shows. The shooting of rifle experts like Annie Oakley in Buffalo Bill's Wild West Show captured the hearts of a mass American audience. They watched rather than shot.[17] Spectators didn't like the dry competitive shooting so admired by Wingate and Corbin; if anything, they would rather try their hand at the shooting galleries in penny arcades. The sprawl of metropolitan areas made long-range rifle shooting a pastime of the wealthy or a fantasy of the urban lower and middle classes. Unless, of course, you were a hunter. And then the right white male could shoot again, guided by a moral code.

But *The Rifle* was not a magazine for hunters, and its limited audience forced the magazine to change. Hence, *Shooting and Fishing* emerged in 1888, competing with the popular *Forest and Stream*, which catered to hunter-philosophers with interests in natural history, exotic locales like Africa, and the rugged outdoor life. But even with this switch there were troubles, as article after article pointed to the demise of game animals throughout the United States, especially in the western states, where conservation laws were only starting and enforcement was minimal. The loss of deer, elk, and game birds was accelerated by the market hunters, the gunners, the poachers, the miners, and the loggers who shot with wild abandon at anything that moved. Rules for the hunt were promoted because the hunters faced the extinction of what they wanted to hunt. When Wingate traveled to Yellowstone Park in 1886, he suggested that the bored soldiers in the western territories take up competitive rife shooting since the Indian wars were over and the men couldn't hunt for thirty to fifty miles around the forts, so depleted was the wild game. Rifle competition would lift their spirits.[18]

Shooting also had to compete with the new craze in angling that took the wealthy classes by storm. Reading Izaak Walton's meditations and reveries, fly fishermen and -women raised difficult questions about the environment, its pollution, and the disappearance of both fish and game. And there was a boyhood innocence to fishing that appealed to businessmen eager to escape the stress of work. An 1899 illustration in *Shooting and Fishing* showed a well-dressed lawyer sitting behind his desk, dreaming about himself as a boy with rod in hand along the banks of a sleepy river. When Arthur Corbin Gould died in

1903, an article in *Shooting and Fishing* pointed out that he had become an active member of the Nuttall Ornithological Club and had risen "above the level of the sportsman to whom the fowls of the air and beasts of the field are only things to be killed."[19]

Articles in *Shooting and Fishing* discouraged hunters from taking pride in the number of kill—the body count—but they still applauded the trophy count: the largest fish, the largest deer, the largest elk. The white, enlightened hunter must still have a means to compete and to display his prowess, if not by numbers then by sheer weight and size. Africa was often the backdrop for these trophy hunts.

And then there were the endless temptations to buy the new sporting equipment that fueled the magazine and its ads. *Shooting and Fishing* reported in detail on the "extravagant expositions" for sportsmen at Madison Square Garden that started in 1895. A "veritable fairyland to lovers of outdoor sport," the show held major exhibitions by Winchester, Marlin, Remington, Colt, Union Metallic Cartridge company, J. Stevens Arms and Tool Co., and E. C. and Schultz Powder Companies.[20] At the Winchester exhibit, the potential buyer could also look inside a mutoscope and watch two men shoot at targets that flew through the air, a breathtaking piece of invention that would soon be replaced by guns-blazing movies about the Wild West.

One 1896 illustration in *Shooting and Fishing* before the Christmas rush to buy presents pictures it well. A young man stands in front of two stores with a wad of bills in his hand. On his right is the Boot and Shoe shop with a string of women's and children's shoes dangling on the wall. Next to it is the Guns & Fishing Tackle store with its line of rifles and shotguns displayed. His choice is difficult, and unlike wealthier sportsmen, his cash is limited. What will it be? Guns or shoes? The illustration is titled, "A Great Temptation."

Into this shifting gun culture beset with shopping choices and competing sports, a single man appeared who would take over much of the public discourse about national need to train worthy riflemen. Just in the nick of time, when rifle ranges were disappearing, Teddy Roosevelt helped out with the creation of the National Board for the Promotion of Rifle Practice in 1903. Rifles would now be distributed by the government for use at civilian ranges, helping out schools, colleges, and civilian rifle clubs. Civilians outside the state militias would continue the tradition of the citizen-soldier. Rifle practice had found its new champion.

Roosevelt had made his fame as a military man, what Sarah Watts has called the "cowboy soldier," in a sense combining the persona of Buffalo Bill and the citizen-soldier rifleman.[21] Riding with his flamboyant Rough Riders to national fame, Roosevelt praised his Winchester rifles during the Spanish American War in Cuba. His image as a buckskin-clad hunter, a cowboy hero, and the lieutenant colonel of the Rough Riders translated into power at the polls and boosted Winchester sales. Roosevelt was a great fan of Winchester rifles in particular and had praised their use in his writings, though he was also quick to add, as he did in his *Ranch Life and the Hunting Trail,* that it's "the man behind the gun that makes the difference. An inch or two in trajectory or a second or two in rapidity of fire is as nothing compared to sureness of eye and steadiness of hand."[22]

This new, virulent form of masculinity that Roosevelt embodied was tempered by a naturalist moral code. As Daniel Justin Herman has discussed in *Hunting and the American Imagination,* in the 1880s and '90s, hunter-politicians of all political persuasions from Congress, the Senate, and the presidency found in hunting an ethical code to advocate manly virtues, gentility, and even progressive politics.[23] Hunter-politicians like Theodore Roosevelt, James Garfield, and Grover Cleveland held often passionate conservation beliefs that resulted in early wildlife and game laws and management strategies. Pushing for game and forest preserves to counter the capitalist development, hunter-philosopher-politicians presented themselves as humane advocates for nature.

When Teddy Roosevelt went on his famous safari to Africa in 1909, he sailed with a bevy of naturalists. Roosevelt shot while they collected, sending back thousands of mammals, birds, reptiles, and fish. The great white hunter walked in the tracks of British colonialism, buoyed by a sense of his own virtue and confident of his prowess with a rifle. In *African Game Trails,* Roosevelt confidently wrote, "The Winchester did admirably with lions, giraffes, elands, and smaller game, and, as will be seen, with hippos. For heavy game like rhinoceros and buffaloes, I found that for me personally the heavy Holland was unquestionably the proper weapon."[24]

These sensational stories of Roosevelt's exploits would soon fade beneath the sirens of war. After Arthur Corbin died, *Shooting and Fishing* became *Arms and the Man,* a vigorous advocate for the National Guard and civilian rifle clubs. Anxious debates about America's readiness for war filled its pages as conflicts in Europe and the Mexican Revolution erupted. Once World War I neared, civilian rifle clubs faced a crisis about their relationship to the citizen soldiers of the state militias, now called the National Guard. Even though civilian rifle clubs doubled in number during and after World War I, their patriotic thunder as part of a select civilian core had been abridged by federal administrative control over state militias. There were even alarms that after the National Defense Act of 1916, the National Guard and its preservation of the citizen-soldier ideal would completely vanish. And with that ideal gone, what would guide the civilian rifleman?

The U.S.–Mexico borderlands would test some of these conflicts. In the years before the United States entered World War I, the Mexican Revolution spilt over into towns in Texas, New Mexico, and Arizona. Regular military and state militia were mobilized, and civilian rifle clubs wanted part of the action. In the July 6, 1916, issue of *Arms and the Man*, the first issue officially owned by the National Rifle Association, the lead story's headline was "The N. R. A. Has Border Troubles." Civilian rifle clubs along the border wanted into the action against Pancho Villa, who had crossed the Rio Grande into U.S. territory. The War Department was quick to reply. They concluded that "the panicky state of mind of citizens along the border" made it "inadvisable to place arms in the hands of any bodies of men excepting those who are under the severest discipline."[25] The disbursal of surplus military weapons in civilian rifle clubs that began with the National Board for the Promotion of Rifle Practice was curtailed, and the threat to stop the supply of any arms to civilian rifle clubs erupted into heated debates in Congress.

In effect, civilians were told that they were not citizen-soldiers. To fight, they needed to enlist and submit to discipline and command. With the NRA ownership of *Arms and the Man* and the temporary absorption of the National Guard into the regular military to fight in World War I, civilian shooters lost some of the moral ground that they had as an unofficial "reserve" of fighting men aligned with the state militias. The regular military also became more involved in the supervision of civilian marksmanship programs subsidized by the government.

After 1917, articles in *Arms and the Man* addressed specific civilian concerns: how still to obtain surplus rifles from government programs, how to set up civilian shooting ranges or to lease militia ranges, and how to work with or against local, state, and, increasingly, federal laws drafted to restrict handgun use, especially the Sullivan Law in New York. But the rifleman as the moral standard of the American white male civilian dissipated in the harsh realities of World War I.

In the 1920s and '30s, the civilian shooter had to find other rationales for his moral right to guns, which was no longer associated with the citizen-soldier rhetoric of the state militia. Race riots after World War I in cities like Tulsa, Chicago, and East Saint Louis, in which whites burnt out black neighborhoods, along with the rise of the Second Ku Klux Klan in Northern and Southern cities, made racial conflict a national concern and no longer only a problem of the South. The long drive of temperance movements that led to Prohibition laws stimulated organized crime. And the Great Depression, with its collapse of price stability, agricultural markets, and the stock exchange, forced farmers off the land and created severe urban unemployment.[26] Some labor organizers responded with the intense beliefs of socialism and communism. Ideas about who would control the violence perpetrated by organized crime, labor agitation, and racial conflict, and how, were reflected in the pages of what became *The American Rifleman* in 1924. The practiced rifleman turned to the civil police and a newly created federal agency, the Federal Bureau of Investigation, to find its new heroes. By the 1930s, the civilian shooter could fantasize about himself as a volunteer G-man of the FBI, less a citizen-soldier than a glamorized crime-stopper, using rifle, revolver, or pistol to get the bad guys who threatened the white middle class.

In the 1930s, *The American Rifleman* was also alert to specific political and legislative restraints of firearm use, and in 1932 it created the Legislative Affairs Division to influence the Federal Firearms Act, which had been established to restrict particular guns, such as sawed-off shotguns and fully automatic weapons—what were called "machine guns." A series of infamous bank robberies and kidnappings between 1933 and 1935 by criminals made legendary in newspapers and radio—such as Machine Gun Kelly, Baby Face Nelson, John Dillinger, and the infamous Bonnie and Clyde—entertained the public and raised concerns about crime.[27] Using taxation and interstate commerce laws, the federal government passed firearms legislation in 1934 and 1938 directed against bank robbers, kidnappers, organized crime, and a long list of subversives such as alien enemies, Communists, Anarchists, Fascists, and labor organizers.

In the 1930s, articles in *The American Rifleman* again pumped up the moral and law-abiding stance of its gun owners by aligning them this time with police organizations, offering to help train officers in marksmanship. Still convinced of their superiority in arms, the civilian shooters who the NRA represented changed their previous patronizing attitudes toward the police that were formerly characterized as corrupt, weak, and unable to shoot well, and welcomed the chance to open their ranges to them. Having squared off against police departments in their attempts to weaken handgun legislation, they tried now to mollify the police by starting special shooting competitions for them at their ranges. And they vehemently argued that criminals were on the rampage because the law and politicians intervened in the affairs of the police force. Their vigilante stance approved of increased firepower to civil police but denigrated the political power of lawyers and politicians who would curb its use. Editorials railed against Congress and glorified the actions of an "aroused *armed* citizenry" fighting crime.

1937 articles in *The American Rifleman* argued against federal registration of firearms but supported a series of laws that curbed what they saw as the criminal use of guns. Registration would hurt "reputable business and professional men," leaving criminals free to act, but support for the Federal Bureau of Investigation in its fight against crime was strong, even though the FBI at this point was mainly fighting what they generally classified as "subversives." The 1930s even saw a special column start in the *American Rifleman*, called "Guns vs. Bandits," that highlighted citizens protecting their businesses and homes and joining in the fight against "a thoroughly armed underworld." Swaggering bandits, Negro burglars, and late-night prowlers were all sent running by armed men and women who acted like local police or G-men, warding off and even capturing the bad guys.

Previous military marksmanship training also paid off, and echoes of the citizen-soldier from the state militia can still be found. In one reported incident in Cleveland, a "sharpshooter" drew a revolver from a secret panel in his store and killed one intruder and wounded another. The storeowner, a Mr. Hewett, was reported as having won an Expert-class rifleman's medal as a member of Company G, Second Regiment, New York National Guard.[28] The citizen-soldier was now a mini G-man, a good guy out to get the bad guys, defending his store and the nation.

Riflemen in particular were written about as war heroes, homesteaders, crime avengers, and even proud owners of sparkling new Packard automobiles. The model husband who worked hard for his family and had learned how to shoot responsibly as a young man could work his way up the ladder to Packard ownership. The white male hero as part of a rifle and hunting tradition was seen as a having a birthright in the United

States that had to be passed down through the generations of appropriately respectable white men. Full-color ads by Du Pont claimed that "Your birthright—and your son's birthright—is an abundant game supply . . . made possible by generations of sportsmen who have observed the rules of wise conservation. Do all in your power to pass your birthright on."

The editors of the *American Rifleman* even claimed that its "fraternity of the rifled tube" had a national face. This tribe of riflemen was the heart of the country. "No more diversified groups can be found in any organization of any kind in America. The butcher, the baker, the candlestick maker, doctor, lawyer, merchant chief, northerner, southerner, easterner, westerner— on the firing line you can't tell them one from another and no one tries to." Except of course that they were still all white men with values hewn from the conflicts surrounding citizen soldiers, hunters, and patrician elites.[29]

That the American character from the point of view of an embattled white, middle-class male was at stake in the glorification of the rifleman is an understatement. In 1941, British firearms laws were attacked as anti-American. "Common sense certainly indicates that the effect of a similar law in America would even more quickly cause the impatient American to give up his guns and turn to golf, picture-making, and the stadium seat to watch paid athletes perform. Common sense, based upon history, says that when the men of any nation have given up their arms for a stadium seat, that nation has deteriorated from greatness into futility."[30] Real men still took to the fields with rifles in their hands and trained in sport shooting. Boy scouts, graduates of Camp Perry and civilian marksmanship matches, they were the regulated men of America, not the soft businessmen on the golf course or those unwashed masses in the baseball stadium.

The rhetoric only intensified as the involvement of the United States in World War II approached. In May, the *American Rifleman* ran a "Re-Dedication" editorial that railed against the intellectuals, who for twenty years had undermined national heroes, the philosophy of Main Street, and the need for the "head of the family and his sons" to defend their homes and womenfolk "by force." The enemy were no longer criminals but a list of subversives who "with the foreign doctrine of Communism" sat "sneeringly in chairs of government, education, labor and agriculture to tie the hands of real Americans who surround them. . . ."[31]

One response was to turn the young boy into a regular military man, no longer the citizen-soldier of the state militia, and send him off to war to defend America as an expert rifleman or small-arms expert. "Johnny Jones," the grocery clerk, can become a "1941 type warrior" if he has learned the discipline of the rifle, a mental training in character, a form of initiation into the American mind. Both the public and the military needed to understand that "thoroughly adequate small arms training produced by-products within Johnny Jones about-to-be-a-soldier which will definitely improve his chances of becoming John Jones, first-class fighting man, *regardless of whether his eventual station is behind the butt-plate of a shoulder rifle, the traversing gear of an anti-tank gun or the bombardier's sights of a giant plane*" (italics in original).[32]

In spite of the increased mechanization of war with tanks, air power, and more lethal weapons, the individual trained in the rifle, pistol, or revolver was the standard of the white male American hero. Small arms and the rifle produced men with the right mental attitude, in touch with the past and with such legends as Buffalo Bill, Teddy Roosevelt, and those countless hunters and their sons traversing the fields and farms. Businessmen and clerks by day, they developed the "right stuff" in the rigors of rifle training and shooting game. They learned through the gun how to become the right American male, patriotic and redeemed, free of subversive philosophies and foreign intrigues. In later articles during 1941, the "ancient Anglo-Saxon doctrine that a man's home is his castle" is supported by the love of "old-fashioned American flag-waving." The critics of the war are labeled "Red" as the flags "sweep out a lot of cob-webs from the minds of Americans," especially those "termites" who "prefer to wave the Red Flag."[33]

Any restriction against rifles and handguns in the hands of these manly men became an assault on the heart of America. The civilian who was not a member of the military or the militia, but who shot with the mind of a patriot and was adamantly ready to defend the nation against attack, stood as the ideal American male. Once defense preparations began for World War II, the *American Rifleman* described how the NRA was "closer to American military leaders than any other civilian organization and closer than most to Congressional leaders charged with national defense planning."[34] Citing a special relationship between a civilian organization and a military trust to defend the country, the civilian shooter rose in moral stature; a man already prepared to become a soldier at any moment, he soaked in the glow of the veteran and the citizen-soldier, even if he never enlisted.

The *American Rifleman* continued to promote ways in which rifle and pistol clubs could produce civilian shooters to assist in marksmanship training for the state guard, police and sheriff's departments, officers of the Army, Navy, Marine Corps, and Coast Guard, and as "special deputies under the local Sheriff or as special officers under the local Chief of Police."[35] These true-blue American rifleman would morph into "qualified auxiliary police for emergency duty," ready to control mobs, learn ju-jitsu, and protect the American way.

The civilian rifleman was a patriot ready to lend his weapon to the military and the police. He was a guardian of the nation, always prepared to defend it against internal and external enemies. He was a renewed and redeemed civilian-soldier, operating in society without either the regulation of the military or the militia, but with a mind that treasured their values and aims. He had never left behind his gun and the mentality of the gun for the soft life of those skeptics who defiled the country with their criticisms and subversions. And the civilian rifleman fought to ensure his rightful place in the reality of a changing America. The vigilant American, a member of a select group of white men, was ready for action, even as a vigilante who decided that his law, the law granted him by his moral superiority, his proper training, and his arms was even more just than the laws of the land.

PART TWO

4

START SHOOTING

In April 2002, I visited Reno, Nevada, a gambling town, set close to a rocky plain punctuated by crystal blue. For three days, I lived amidst quarter slots, pawnshops, and sprawling megahotels. Driving into the city from the airport, I saw that the parking lot of the hotel hosting the National Rifle Association's annual convention was filling with RVs. I planned on attending their daylong legal seminar and as many meetings as I could squeeze into the weekend. And most important, I knew I had to show up early to the annual members' meeting if I was going to find a seat up front to watch and listen to Charlton Heston.

A taxi ferried me over to the Silver Legacy and then on to the Reno Sparks Convention Center. My cabbie looked like Willie Nelson. He sped around the streets and filled me in on who he was and how he ended up in Reno. He said he was a Vietnam vet and wanted me to know he'd been in Cambodia in 1960, working the Ho Chi Minh trail for the 18th Airborne. He told me that most Americans didn't know about that early war. He had been an invisible soldier for the U.S.A. and had moved to Reno to get away from government. Restless, he spun around the corners talking about his beat-up buddies living off their disabled-vet checks. He was strung tight.

Settling into the ride, I wasn't ready for his political message. He yanked his head around and shouted. "If our founding fathers were alive today, they would just start shooting— without warning." Just as quickly, he tried to beat a red light. Was he kidding? I didn't say a thing. I sat there trying to look neutral. For a second, I imagined James Madison and Thomas Jefferson locked and loaded, spraying the American populace who dared disobey. Maybe this was cabbie talk, extreme words to cut through the boredom of carrying around sad-sack gamblers. He was hyped on his political message, and I was his captive audience. The way he was driving, I hoped his talk wasn't laced with crystal meth, the recreational drug of the rural West.

The cabbie said he liked driving NRA folks around. He had to remember to renew his membership. I got the impression he was short on cash. Time was running out for America; just start shooting, he repeated. I broke neutrality and asked him if he was kidding. He'd been in Vietnam. Did he really want the founding fathers and their select descendants to transform themselves into a bunch of patriotic Terminators? He shrugged his shoulders and sped on.

Having walked the aisles of more than a dozen gun shows, I was used to hearing about the founding fathers and their wisdom in writing the Second Amendment to the U.S. Constitution. Gun owners had given me hundreds of mini–history lessons as I stood handling their wares. But turning the founding fathers into a pack of armed avengers for freedom plinking off their fellow citizens was over the top even in the hyped rhetoric of the gun-rights world. Anyway, who were they going to start shooting? The cabbie didn't seem to target me in his message. After all, he was driving me to the annual convention of the NRA. He assumed I was one of what he called the "upstanding folks" protecting his right to bear arms. I decided not to tell him I was in town to listen and take notes. He was another reason why I wanted to understand how guns anchored a political movement in the United States. To him I was a patriot. A fellow traveler.

For three days I wandered the halls of the Convention Center in Reno. I met and talked with dozens of participants and listened to their fiery patriotism, which was always backed up by references to the Revolutionary War and quotes from the Bill of Rights, or at least the Second Amendment: that is, the "right to bear arms" amendment. I was told over and over again that eighteenth-century divines like James Madison and Thomas Jefferson had guaranteed them their right to bear arms. The founding fathers confirmed their beliefs; history vindicated them. The Second Amendment to the Constitution bound together the crowds of mainly white, middle-aged men hurrying to grassroots organizational sessions, committee meetings, and seminars.

At first, I was surprised at both their certainty and of their repeated belief in the past. No squabbling over the meaning of a phrase in the Constitution or the interpretation of an event like the Revolutionary War. The original intent of the documents written before, during, and after our eight-year war with the British was as crystal-clear as the sky above Reno. Even further, democracy rested upon a recognition that the "right to keep and bear arms" was the linchpin of political freedom.

The United States Supreme Court has never interpreted the
Second Amendment as affirming an individual right to own a
gun, despite repeated attempts by gun-rights groups to have the
Court rule on this issue.[1] But the U.S. Constitution and the Bill
of Rights are not only legal documents, they are political documents that people are free to interpret.[2] The National Rifle Association and the other gun-rights groups in the United States
have promoted their fundamental-rights position with persuasion, conviction, and an understanding of how emotionally and
financially invested many Americans are in their guns. Most of
the people I know believe that the Second Amendment guarantees them the personal right to own a gun. Even fellow historians and lawyers I have known urged me to forget about the
Second Amendment. Michael Moore in *Bowling for Columbine*
readily agreed. He didn't want his film mucked up with legal
debates and merely nodded his head in consent with the gun-
rights position.

Rhetorically, the gun-rights movement has claimed direct
descent from the Revolutionary period. It has claimed the
founding fathers and the founding documents to build a vision
of the United States and its model citizens. The founding fathers are, of course, always good to have on your side, even
if the historical situations they survived and shaped were en-
trenched in conflict, compromise, and ambiguity. How the dynamic and turbulent actions of that period and the writings
produced from that time are alive in our imaginations is the
stuff of politics, not only of law.

For an entire day, I attended the NRA law seminar. One
speaker urged the audience to "bring back the Second Amendment to its proper historic place." Others focused on cases
pending in the courts that would restrict my individual gun
rights. In the hallway outside the seminar, someone handed me

a plea, trying to raise money for a legal defense fund for a person charged with violating the now-defunct assault-weapons ban. The broadside pulled no punches. "The left wing media, the gun grabbing politicians, communists, international socialists and traitors want to make an example of this outstanding **patriotic American Citizen**, so that all other patriotic Americans will be **afraid to own personal firearms for protection!**"

The volume was high.

Some people I know don't think much about the Second Amendment. "What amendment?" they say, looking at me sheepishly and trying to run by the usual suspects. "Freedom of speech and religion? Is it one of those?" They are the political freeloaders that some gun-rights advocates shake their heads about. Many, they insist, are even gun owners without a clue about the political meaning of what they have in a shoebox in their closet or locked away in a safe in the back bedroom. Freeloaders. Sleeping-Beauty citizens. The mission is to wake them up to the historic meaning of the Second Amendment. I walked by signs, booths, books, and organizations dedicated to this pursuit. The NRA even publishes a magazine called *America's 1st Freedom*, which switches the order of the Bill of Rights: the Second Amendment was the first freedom upon which all other freedoms in the United States rested. I bought a heavy tome with pages of political writings from the revolutionary period, stuffed with quotes from the Anti-Federalists who waged a war of words with James Madison and Alexander Hamilton. I lugged it around to the meetings at the NRA convention and read passages between sessions. [3]

The Second Amendment, called a military amendment by many historians, sounds fairly awkward to twenty-first-century ears. "A well-regulated militia, being necessary to a free state, the right of the people to keep and bear arms, shall not be infringed." That's it. All you get is one sentence. A sentence with a big *not* in it.

In the fierce debates over gun rights and gun control, a cleaver often divides this sentence in half. The first half, claimed mainly by some historians, legal scholars, and the Supreme Court, underscores the "militia" reference. The second half, claimed by gun-rights organizations, their attorneys, other historians and legal scholars, and the arms industry, stakes out the "people" part of the sentence.

Law journals, historical studies, and gun magazines debate and claim victory for their points of view. There are even courses in law schools using the Second Amendment as a way to give budding lawyers a glimpse into the world of legal conflict. The fight is usually over whether the amendment guarantees an individual right, or a collective right as a member of a state militia, to own a gun. If it does guarantee an individual right, owning a gun becomes a political act of fundamental importance to citizenship, protected by the Constitution, and a forum in which to advocate a set of political beliefs for gun owners. If it doesn't, then gun ownership is downgraded to the practical concerns of self-defense, recreation, and crime. Guns are not protected to the extent that freedom of speech is by the Bill of Rights.

Most people I talked with at the convention quickly told me that they have an absolute individual right to own a gun. They didn't say they had a right to protect themselves. No, they had a constitutional right to own a gun. And for many, this right was equal if not surpassing the First Amendment, freedom of speech. Some in Reno even went a step further: the Second Amendment was the "teeth" of the Bill of Rights. They were brave citizen enforcers of the Bill of Rights. Take the words of a chemist I interviewed who two years before had joined a local grassroots organization of the NRA. "You must be responsible for your own safety, life, liberty, and pursuit of happiness." The gun was the means. Sitting in his small university office filled with student lab reports, he said history was a "hobby" for him. With gun in hand, the individual citizen guaranteed the enforcement of the Bill of Rights. He would protect my rights with his gun. The word "people" in the Second Amendment meant each and every individual in the United States.[4]

What about the militia references? I would often ask. Not relevant, most would say. They would repeat to me the second half of the amendment, ". . . the right of the people to keep and bear arms, shall not be infringed." Some gun-rights organizations have stopped citing the first half of the sentence altogether. They begin with "the right of the people to keep and bear arms shall not be infringed," dropping the comma between "arms" and "shall."

But this deliberate erasure of the first half of the amendment would have disturbed many of our founding fathers. A well regulated militia meant a citizen's army composed completely of white men between the ages of eighteen and forty-five who were under the authority of officers appointed by the states and training prescribed by Congress. If anything, the legal case for individual rights in relation to the Second Amendment came much later, after the fiery war between the states and the writing of the Fourteenth Amendment that was used to protect individuals from repressive state governments. But that was not the point in Reno. The point was to legitimize a twentieth-century political movement through the language of rights from the eighteenth-century. Perhaps that is why the gun debate in the United States is so fierce. If the Second Amendment isn't about granting the individual a fundamental right to own a gun, then the gun owner is only a hunter, or a target shooter, or someone who needs a form of personal protection. In the end, he is only a gun owner. But with the Second Amendment, he is a "freedom fighter."

But what about the first half of the sentence, discarded like an empty shoebox? Those two phrases sit on the tongue awkwardly: "A well-regulated militia, being necessary to a free state." To eighteenth-century Americans, these words had concrete historical meaning. The standing armies of the king, often mercenaries from other countries, could be used against the people ruthlessly. The defense against such a tyrant was an armed and disciplined militia composed of the people, at that time meaning white men of a certain age range. Trust was placed in these men to defend the community and the state. With that trust supposedly came responsibility and regulation, and officers and training were part of the militia experience. The adjective "well-regulated" was not an afterthought because a fear of the unruly, armed mob haunted the essays and letters of the postrevolutionary writers. A point of heated debate at the time was who would choose the officers—the individual states, or the national government? A compromise was hammered out, giving the states "the Appointment of the Officers, and the Authority of training the Militia according to the discipline prescribed by Congress."

Of course, that was an ideal. In reality, many local militias, especially volunteer units, elected their own officers. They were networks of kin based in specific towns.[5] And they could and did cause trouble for the state and national governments. Especially in the western lands of the new republic, militia groups rebelled against their state governments and heated up the violence among Indian tribal groups and encroaching settlers.[6] And then there was that other disturbing reality of early America: since only white men were mentioned in the 1792 Uniform Militia Act, militias were used to keep in check the restless actions of enslaved Africans, even though slaves and freed blacks were periodically enlisted to serve if the situation made it necessary.

The writers of the Second Amendment understood these explosive dangers. They were themselves actors in the revolution, and many found the word "well-regulated" to their purpose in a post-revolutionary and nation-building world. Preserve the right of the people to defend themselves against tyrants, but insist that they submit to discipline, training, and command. A check on the excesses of national government, and a check on the unruly actions of rogue individuals and factions.

Militias were unpopular with a key political leader at the time. Alexander Hamilton thought they would be "a real grievance to the people and a serious public inconvenience and loss." What shopkeeper or farmer would keep his arms in working condition and train enough to be of practical use? Hamilton pushed for the development of a navy and worked hard to organize the military. Having served with Washington as an aide and a soldier during the Revolutionary War, he believed that only a national army could get the job done. Soldiering required expertise acquired over time. He was impatient with all this talk of militias. But other political leaders felt strongly that free citizens had a civic duty to serve in the state militias. They were obligated to serve. To be precise: this ideal was lost in the early decades of the American nation.

As a people, we no longer require compulsory militia service of our citizens. We use a professional and volunteer military or a volunteer National Guard to protect us. That is why many historians and legal scholars consider the Second Amendment archaic. The political vision of universal conscription in state militias has vanished. It belongs to our revolutionary past, a vision of a republic and its citizens abandoned.[7]

The Second Amendment is no longer a well-formed or well-regulated collection of words: the tensions in the sentence have exploded into warring camps. At the annual meeting of the NRA, the lines could not have been more sharply drawn. Gun owners expressed the belief that they were surrounded by a mob of gun grabbers threatening their basic constitutional right. One speaker pleaded that the state of California sink into the sea. He lived in the "belly of the beast," a state that tried to outlaw the .50 caliber rifle (and three years later succeeded). California, he said, was a state trying to tax each bullet, a state that had run out of town the largest gun show in the United States, and a state intent on disarming its citizens.

As is always the case, these emotions came to a head when Charlton Heston walked onstage. The sight of his fragile body, his slow and hesitant steps, silenced the crowd. He paused and looked around, grabbing the podium for balance. Then he gave them what they wanted. He raised above his head a Winchester rifle and repeated the five sacred words: "From my cold, dead hands," words that had become his hallmark greeting to his adoring fans. Shouts, hoots, and applause filled the hall packed with 5,000 people. He stood with his rifle held high in defiance of the gun grabbers. Ready to defend the Second Amendment. Ready to defend American freedom.

What followed were sermons that echoed Heston's gesture. There was no compromise with an evil deep within American society. The "enemies" in the United States had a "singular hatred" for the ideals of freedom. Because there were "no flavors of freedom," the fight of the NRA was a moral crusade. There was no middle ground. "You are either with us or against us."

The white-haired man in suspenders sitting next to me pounded his knee and called out, "Damn right!" The Arizona man sitting behind me, dressed in his best Cabela's outdoors wear, peppered the sermons with rapid-fire comments on how America was trying to take everything away from him. He was mad about property taxes and worthless regulations. The room was rocking with emotion.

No one at the annual meeting talked about the need to start shooting. They may have had caches of guns at home, but they talked grassroots organizing, ballot initiatives, and media tactics. They had the guns, but they trusted the ballot. And they had won by throwing money, time, and labor into federal and state political campaigns in 2000 and 2002. And they would win again at the polls in 2004.

5

READING *AMERICAN RIFLEMAN*

A t gun shows I always look for old copies of the *American
Rifleman*, searching in their pages for the reasons why and
how guns have entered our politics during the twentieth century. Its editorials, ads, and essays are a repository of political
values attached to weapons. Sometimes I can find stacks of
yellowing issues from the 1950s, and at one show I bought a
two-feet thick pile of old magazines. After World War II the
American Rifleman became a hefty shopping guide for recreational shooting and hunting. Over the years, the NRA has
added more magazines: *American Hunter, America's 1st Freedom,* and *Woman's Outlook.* Every month for the last three
years, I have found in my mailbox *America's 1st Freedom,* a slick,
ad-filled blast at liberals; renegade English-speaking countries
with strict gun laws, like England and Australia; and gun own-

ers who hunt, shoot, or use guns in something other than the "right" political frame of mind. The covers caricature people like George Soros and John Kerry while heaping praise on Charlton Heston, Dick Cheney, and Wayne LaPierre.

The stack of discarded magazines from the 1950s that I carried home from one show featured sentimental images of fathers and sons walking the fields, bird hunting or learning the technical features of new cartridges, scopes, or firearms. After World War II, returning veterans took to the woods for recreation and membership in the NRA tripled in the single year between 1945 and 1946. In the *American Rifleman*, "how to" articles on hunting introduced a generation of men to the pastime of shooting deer and game birds, often with the same moral rhetoric of earlier years but without its passion for animals or the environment. Recreational hunting had been increasing for the middle class since the increased availability of the automobile in the 1920s. And by 1945 almost 25 percent of American men hunted as opposed to 7 percent in 1996.[1] The vast majority of these hunters, up to 95 percent today, has been and continues to be white men.

Curiosity about the guns used in the war and the booty brought back from the war, dozens of books on historical guns, and surplus cash spurred a postwar wave of gun collecting for investment and fun. War heroes and their weapons gave a glow to the gun owners, and columns about "bandits" dropped away. One man I interviewed, who said he overlooked everything else but the issue of gun ownership when he voted, had begun to collect German Mauser pistols in the 1950s. There were "so many wonderful weapons" to collect after World War II.[2] The elitist recreational sojourns of Teddy Roosevelt–like heroes with their African safaris still dotted the pages of the *American Rifleman*, but now the average white guy takes center stage as he is instructed on how to build a shooting range, how to hunt, and how his fellow veterans performed with honor under fire.

In 1948, an "exhibit of arms" began the annual NRA corporate meeting, involving dealers, manufacturers, NRA-affiliated gun-collector organizations, and branches of the Armed Services. After 1945, besides articles on hunting, historical gun collecting, and military guns from World Wars I and II, the magazine included regular columns on technical firearms information, court cases often involving accidental shootings and liability issues, and information on where to target-shoot. The magazine also continued its pages of classified ads, called "The Arms Chest" through which gun owners and manufacturers could circulate. guns for resale, trade, refurbishing, and collecting.

The *American Rifleman* supplied hunters and gun collectors with feature articles on the hunting of bear, elk, deer, and birds along with historical articles on colonial and frontier arms. Competitive sport shooting was kept alive at the edges of the magazine through reports on matches and top individual and team winners, especially service marksmanship by U.S. military teams. In these post–World War II years, the *American Rifleman* sustained its reporting and promotion of competitive rifle and pistol events through reporting on civilian, military, and Olympic matches.

Changes in the law as they affected shooter-sportsmen were discussed in reports on permits for shooting ranges, minimum age limits for purchase of guns, prohibition of hunting on posted lands, and restrictions on what guns were appropriate for hunting. And the controversies about gun shows were addressed. By 1937, the Ohio Gun Collectors Association had already organized, and other groups followed, often holding gun shows to display, swap, and sell historical firearms.[3] By 1961, there were sixty gun collector organizations affiliated with the National Rifle Association. Gun shows were often groups of serious collectors who met in closed sessions, listening to lectures and technical information on historical guns. And they saw themselves as good guys who kept alive the American heritage of firearms. They believed that gun collecting was patriotic, connecting gun ownership to the revolutionary and pioneer past of the United States.

Today, the Ohio Gun Collectors Association lays it on thick when it describes its history. In 1937, members would display personal gun collections for educational purposes alone. Nothing was for sale. They merely wanted to find time and space to be among those who "spoke the language of the true firearms collector." Even more important, firearms collecting carried political meaning, creating a "common bond" that provided the glue for national identity. Guns and gun collecting were at the heart of remembering who we were as a people: "Without firearms we would not today be free men and women."[4]

In the 1950s, commercial gun shows became more popular, and with them came controversy. To dispel fears about guns in the places where these shows were held, organizers were encouraged to hand out brochures on the American firearms heritage and why Americans own, shoot, and collect guns. In 1961, the *American Rifleman* highly recommended that codes of ethics and conduct should be observed and enforced at both commercial and collector shows. Further, local celebrities and individuals from the media should be invited to make gun ownership seem reasonable and respectable.[5] It was one thing to carry on about collecting historical guns as a way to preserve and connect with nationalistic interpretations of the past, but how could the need to buy any gun look patriotic? Commercial sales swamped these historical gun sales, as gun shows gradually became gun markets where patriotic purchasers competed with ordinary consumers who might even want guns for illegal purposes.[6]

Historical guns could easily find a place in this heated gun market, and remakes from several theaters of historical conflicts were manufactured. The Cold War ideology of the 1950s brought back frontier guns and the clear moral code of the cowboy, to reassure Americans of their righteousness after the horrific carnage of World War II, including the use of atomic weapons in Japan.[7] And with this movement came movie stars who, like Buffalo Bill, could advertise specific guns and promote sales. John Wayne and Roy Rogers found their way into gun ads. The Western rifleman as frontier hero was reinserted into American culture through dozens of popular prime-time television series. Six-shooters appeared with greater frequency, as the frontier became again an imagined arena for male prowess with expert weapons leveled against simple evil targets. Nineteen-sixties ads for remakes of frontier revolvers dotted the pages of the *American Rifleman*, feeding the white male consumer's need to buy and collect military guns and frontier-style weapons.[8] The cultural staying power of the Western was enormous; it was a lie about the western United States that, as Larry McMurtry has pointed out, everyone wanted to believe. By the 1990s, the *American Rifleman* could run an ad about a new John Wayne Western Commemorative as the "Gun that Won the Westerns." Movies, not history, stimulated the buying game.[9]

The gun culture found in the pages of the *American Rifleman* was monolithic on one level, involving mainly white men, but diverse on another, as guns crossed over into a range of sports from hunting to competitive shooting, and from collecting historical guns from the Revolutionary and later periods to buying the latest remake of a Colt Peacemaker and ogling the military rifles used by the Japanese or Germans in the recently ended World War. And some men crossed over as shooters, hunters, and collectors, and thus as avid consumers of what was new and available to buy. In the 1950s and '60s, the magazine continued to include more articles on hunting and the effects on shooter-sportsmen of changes in the law and land use, even discussing the liability issues of accidental shootings during hunts, in the home, and at gun stores.[10]

What readers of this magazine had in common was a sense that they were using guns responsibly. They were not buying guns to commit crimes. They were buying and using guns for sport, recreation, historical collection, or plain consumerism, and they drew upon the language of the frontier, hunting, and previous wars to stress their morality and justify their purchases.

Yet these ninety-year-old beliefs, with their roots in the messy aftermath of the Civil War, crashed against a wall in the early 1960s when white men and white racism were identified publicly as the greatest cause of violence in the United States. The civil and political unrest of the late 1950s and '60s challenged white America to question systemic racial inequality, militarism, corporate capitalism, and violence. Labor unrest and racial inequality could no longer be simply brushed aside as the work of foreign immigrants, hoodlums, and subversives. After the assassinations of President John F. Kennedy, Dr. Martin Luther King, Jr., and U.S. Senator Robert F. Kennedy, the government and many universities issued report after report that pointed to a web of complicity by white America that denied African Americans and other minorities jobs, housing, education, health care, and legal representation. What was worse, the police and the legal system were directly implicated in the violence of the cities. And white vigilantes only added to the terror, with a wave of attacks on civil-rights workers and burnings of black churches.

The relative calm of these postwar years started to crumble, as the civil-rights movement changed the way in which white Americans thought about themselves. It was the social change of the 1960s, as much as the hated Gun Control Act of 1968, that shaped the political reasons for why these "honest citizens" needed their guns.[11] The political battles over guns began in earnest in the 1960s and only increased in volume until the National Rifle Association itself was shaken to its roots. By 1977, the NRA had erupted in what some writers have called the "Cincinnati Revolt," and a virulent politics of gun ownership emerged with an anger and self-righteousness backed up by the United State Constitution.[12]

But it would take time and work. In the seventeen-year period between 1960 and 1977, gun advocates writing articles in the *American Rifleman* fumbled to reach a high moral ground from which to defend gun owners and finally found rhetorical security in the Second Amendment to the Constitution. The shift in these years brought a dramatic return to the language of the founding fathers to justify why men—usually white men— needed to control what they owned, and why they owned guns. Ultimately, no one—no person, no law, not even a government— had a right to interfere with the moral prerogative of the individual to buy and own weapons. That prerogative rested only with the "law-abiding citizen."

The invocation of the Second Amendment was glaringly absent before the early 1960s. In the pages of *The Rifle, Shooting and Fishing,* and *Arms and the Man,* the Second Amendment was entangled with a host of legal technicalities about state militias, the federal control of the National Guard, and bitter debates between the states and the federal government about funding and the selection of officers. These dusty disagreements—which created passionate appeals by the volunteer citizen-soldiers of the state militias at the end of the nineteenth century—no longer gave much justification for civilian gun ownership in the 1960s.

In the *American Rifleman*, the first stirrings of change occurred in scattered editorials in the early 1960s arguing that individual right must prevail against "public interest" and that the individual must become "eternally vigilant" to protect the right to keep and bear arms.[13] Even worse, Americans were falling for the "Big Government pattern." The Liberty Bell of 1776 has been "supplanted by the weak tinkle of bells chained around the necks of individuals seeking security under the domination of the State."[14] In editorials, the NRA insisted on its historical mission of training citizen-soldiers, members of organized militia (that is, the National Guard), and "reputable citizens."

By 1964, a more serious analysis of the Second Amendment and its legal connection to state militias began. Unfortunately for the cause, these articles on the Second Amendment were fairly complex and did not offer much rhetorical fire for a simple and direct evocation of the constitutional right. In 1964, an article by Judge Bartlett Rummel traced the complicated legal issues of the Second Amendment and asked for a more direct ruling from the Supreme Court that would guarantee individual rights to gun owners. Rummel fell back on the position that the right to bear arms was a basic, natural right, and he wrote that it was more than a "feeble hope" that the highest court in the land would finally recognize and legitimize gun ownership through the Bill of Rights.[15]

But a gun ad that year said it much better. In 1964, Redfield Gun Sight Company, a popular manufacturer of mounts and telescopic sights, simply said: "We are legally and morally right in opposing bad legislation through the Second Amendment of the Constitution."[16] Simple. Who cares what the Supreme Court says or has said or might say? We, the people, claim the right. Now, that's rhetorical power.

In 1968, the Kerner Commission singled out white racism as a major factor in the urban and domestic violence of the United States, stating, "What white Americans have never fully understood—but what the Negro can never forget—is that white society is deeply implicated in the ghetto. White institutions created it, white institutions maintain it, and white society condones it." Stated by a group of moderates, not liberals, these words challenged basic ideas about the United States that were rejected by conservative politicians on the right.[17] The commission's report became a bestseller that is still controversial today.

Further, the Kerner report listed police practices, overreaction, abuse, and racism as contributing to the explosive situation in the urban ghettos. In the late 1960s, investigations by think tanks, federal commissions, and universities into crime and violence in the United States produced a slew of reports on what policy changes were needed to make America safe. Employment, education, and housing, not crime, were cited as the major causes of violence in the ghettoes, and the police were not neutral players. Recommendations for the training and recruitment of minorities, and for appropriate resources, were advocated. The Kerner Commission attached a strong warning: "The Commission believes there is a grave danger that some communities may resort to the indiscriminate and excessive use of force . . . The Commission condemns moves to equip police departments with mass destruction weapons, such as automatic rifles, machine guns, and tanks. Weapons which are designed to destroy, not control, have no place in densely populated urban communities."[18]

President Lyndon Johnson's Great Society reforms, especially the Office of Economic Opportunity, began to address economic and political shifts in policy that confronted urban infrastructure, housing, and jobs for the poor and minorities. However, the Omnibus Crime Bill of 1967 and the Gun Control Act of 1968, bipartisan legislation supported by the National Rifle Association, granted the Federal Government expanded powers to regulate firearms—formerly a power reserved to states. The final report of the National Commission on the Causes and Prevention of Violence came out in 1970, when Richard Nixon was already President. It cast a wide net over social causes, going beyond poverty to television, drugs, youth culture, and the availability of firearms. Handguns were singled out as the most likely crime weapon, and the efficacy of the use of guns for self-defense in the home as a deterrent against crime was considered unproven and perhaps even nonexistent. Restrictive licensing of handguns was proposed and a comprehensive look at the "patchwork" of municipal, state, and federal firearms regulations encouraged.

This systemic approach to curbing violence was overwhelmed by high-pitched alarms about crime in the United States. An *American Rifleman* editorial in 1968 declared that the problem in the United States was not firearms, but crime; that "an increasing number of lawless individuals in our lax and permissive society commit crimes with guns."[19] Analysis of the social, political, and economic conflicts in the United States and, especially, the issue of white racism was cast aside. Any individual complicity with the conditions that necessitated the civil-rights movement and the conflicts over foreign policy in

Vietnam was denied. The editorial also declared that gun regulation would "betray behind their backs thousands of young Americans now obeying orders to die gun in hand, if necessary, to halt Communism in distant Vietnam."[20]

Guns were innocent, just like the good hunters, sport shooters, collectors, and consumers who owned them. They were not to blame. Nothing was wrong with good guys owning guns. The good guys had nothing to do with violence in America. The bad guys with guns were to blame. The criminals and the lenient judicial system that kept them on the street were to blame. "Don't blame me" was the outcry from many gun owners. "I'm good. And don't blame my gun." They rejected any interpretation that pointed to a systemic pattern of injustice in the United States. They simply weren't involved. And they didn't have to change anything they believed or did.

In the 1960s, the gun debate entered a quagmire of statistics and insults that replaced any discussion of the systemic issues of violence in the society with the single issue of gun ownership by individuals. The process of social change was bogged down in endless arguments about registration, confiscation, and regulation of firearms through federal, state, and municipal laws, statues, and codes. Even defining what a gun was became a dramatic political event. Reasonable discussions about regulation as opposed to infringement simply could not occur in this climate, in which guns themselves were part of an imagined and defended identity that was threatened by increasing racial and political violence in the country.

The only people who benefited from this emotional fusion of innocence with arms were naive white patriots, racists, and people who were enraged by the criticisms of the United States that found their way into public life during the 1960s. And, of course, many arms manufacturers. To the armed citizen, the war in Vietnam was necessary to protect free enterprise from the marauding Communists intent on global domination. And the shift in social values urged by millions of black and white Americans was the bogus propaganda of socialists and big-government proponents.

The blame game heated up, as firearms became a convenient scapegoat for politicians who preferred to focus on their regulation than on changing the way in which the United States educated its citizens, developed the economy of its cities, or ran its political system. Gun debates froze politicians into warring camps who hurled insults. But there were reasons for the public need to face how society would regulate guns. More guns— and more-lethal guns—had begun to circulate in American society after World War II.[21]

Further, three factors contributed to calls for increased legal control over gun ownership in the 1960s: the number of cheap surplus gun imports flooding the American markets from the previous war, the availability of guns through mail-order sales, and the more-lethal types of weapons produced and under production by both domestic and foreign arms manufacturers. Since guns are durable consumer goods, these technological and distribution changes affected the market, often flooding it with specific firearms.[22]

The *American Rifleman* now made crime its teaser, glorifying the actions of armed individuals. Early in the 1960s, a sidebar called the Armed Citizen appeared in the *American Rifleman*: a crime blotter featuring ordinary Americans stopping crime in either their business or home through firing or brandishing a gun. By 1970, the Armed Citizen was featured as a column that had increased in size to two thirds of a page. Today in NRA's magazine, *America's 1st Freedom*, this same column is a full-page condensation of newspaper reports billed as "true stories of the right to keep and bear arms," and readers are urged to call in their "firsthand 'Armed Citizen' experience." The hero in this column is the crime-stopping American who single-handedly thwarts an assault, robbery, or rape.

Crime as a topic began to appear in more pages of the *American Rifleman* during the late 1960s, with statistical arguments about murder and the need for law enforcement, not new laws. Senators Thomas J. Dodd from Connecticut and Edward Kennedy from Massachusetts were labeled as anti-NRA politicians who confused Americans by wanting to regulate firearms, not criminals. In the early 1970s, a new political language urged gun owners to protest gun laws through their voting rights. One of the provisions of the 1968 gun act that irritated gun owners was the requirement that .22 rimfire ammunition used in rifles and its complementary .22 ammunition for handguns could only be purchased by people who showed a form of identification. Since .22 ammunition is significantly cheaper than most, it is commonly used for target practice and to improve shooting skills in general, whether for competitive shooting, recreational shooting, or hunting. An editorial in the February, 1970 issue urged buyers of .22 ammunition to use their voter registration card and make the statement that gun owners were organizing to protect their access to guns and ammunition. In the following month, this political action was reinforced by the NRA's moral claim that its members had "nothing to fear" and "nothing for which to apologize." They were "men banded together for good purposes in an honorable association."[23]

Since the nineteenth century, gun manufacturers have known that they had to make gun ownership moral, either through romantic tales of frontier conquest, national masculinity, or the legacy of hunting. All these moral positions were under attack in the 1960s, especially when an understanding of racism became crucial to confronting and solving violence in the United States. The Armed Citizen was an early rebuttal to criticism leveled against gun owners; it reduced these critiques to the single issue of crime.

What emerged by 1973 was a concerted effort to reclaim the moral right to own guns and to find rationales for gun ownership that reassured gun owners that they were patriotic citizens and honorable men—in fact, American heroes. In 1971, Barry Goldwater was the keynote speaker at the Centennial Members Banquet held at the annual meeting of the NRA. In his speech, he cautioned that Americans had forgotten about the constitutional guarantee that "Americans, free Americans, shall have the right to bear arms."[24] And he praised our "forefathers, those proud and God-fearing pioneers who tamed this nation."[25] The Second Amendment needed to be remembered. It needed to be resurrected for these white civilians. They needed a massive cultural pat on the back to tell them they were indeed the core of the nation.

During this time, the magazine still catered to hunters and sport shooters with enthusiastic articles about the sport-shooting facility that the NRA was going to build in Colorado Springs as part of a general training center for Olympic athletes; other long articles appeared on the subjects of ballistics and historical guns. But in 1971, an event occurred that helped to increase the tensions within the NRA. In June of that year, when Alcohol, Tobacco, and Firearms (ATF) agents with the Montgomery County Police raided the apartment of Kenyon F. Ballew, a lifetime NRA member, shots were exchanged and Ballew fell to the floor with a head wound. The revolver in Ballew's hand had been shot once, and Ballew's shooting was declared an act of self-defense: an ATF officer and two policemen who had fired a total of eight times into the apartment and at Ballew were all acquitted.

The ardent reactionary William Loeb, then editor of the *Manchester Union Leader*, whose father had been secretary to Teddy Roosevelt, and who had been a member of the NRA Directors since 1969 and was Chair of its Public Relations Committee, pumped up the volume by calling the ATF officers "Treasury Gestapo." The Ballew case became a cause célèbre in the *American Rifleman* in denouncing the Gun Control Act of 1968 and its enforcement agency, ATF, which was under the supervision of the Department of the Treasury. The image of a white man shot by government agents in his home helped dissipate the charge of white racism's connection to systemic violence. White gun owners were the new victims.

To Loeb, a white gun owner besieged by ATF agents became the showcase victim of gun regulation. Ballew was charged with having possession of a sawed-off version of a stock and barrel, illegal under the 1934 National Firearms Act and a destructive device as defined by the 1968 Gun Control Act. Ironically, during the 1960s, there were numerous charges against the FBI in its surveillance of civil-rights and anti–Vietnam War organizers and its infiltration of many nonviolence organizations with the intent of disrupting their activities. Yet, instead of finding common cause in the abuses of government agencies, the Ballew case legitimized an increasingly reactionary form of political discourse by journalists like Loeb who worked to undermine any discussion of progressive economic or political change in the United States.

By 1972, Loeb and the Public Relations Committee he headed were hunting for a big moral stick with which to defend their position. Loeb turned to the Bill of Rights and urged that a study be made of the relationship between the First and Second Amendments that could be released to the press.[26] Faced with the fact that the Second Amendment had never been interpreted by the United States Supreme Court as a guaranteed right of individual civilian gun ownership, the NRA made a concerted effort to change how this amendment was interpreted and perceived by the public. An *American Rifleman* article in March 1973 accused the court of making a "grave mistake."[27] Other articles followed, debating the legalisms surrounding the history of the Second Amendment until finally the armed citizen was simply declared protected by the Bill of Rights.[28]

By 1976, the political rhetoric had gained momentum and the bicentennial year brought out a new NRA campaign called the Rally to Arms, "designed to enroll defenders of the right to keep and bear arms" in numbers equal "to the ranks of the patriots who fought in the American Revolution."[29] A campaign called Project Freedom was started to help build the "ranks of NRA's New Patriot Army." A massive membership drive was launched, and contributors who solicited between five and twenty new members during the campaign could earn medallions with appointments as captain, major, or colonel. In the previous year, a political-action arm of the NRA, the Institute for Legislative Action, had been launched under the leadership of Executive Director Harlon B. Carter.

In the following year, Carter would successfully oust the old leadership of the NRA in a battle during the 1977 annual meeting in Cincinnati, referred to as the Cincinnati Revolt. Several people have written about Carter's dramatic seizure of the NRA leadership and the conflict between what Josh Sugarmann calls "the New and Old Guards" in its organization, explaining how Carter's background in the U.S. Border Patrol and the Immigration and Naturalization Service (INS) made him a formidable opponent to those who represented some of the recreational and competitive shooters, hunters, and collectors who were not as interested in turning guns into a political weapon for conservative causes.[30] Leading up to Carter's takeover, eighty staff members had been let go in November 1976, including all of the newly hatched Institute for Legislative Action, headed by Carter. Preparing to move the NRA headquarters to Colorado Springs, the pre-Carter leadership was radically undermining the nascent political mission of the organization, keeping the NRA focused instead on sport-shooting and hunting.

But in 1977, after the dust from the annual meeting had settled, the plans to move the NRA headquarters out of Washington, D.C. to Colorado Springs and the building of an elaborate sports facility were quashed. Instead, the PAC activities of the NRA boomed. And in 1977, new articles on the Second Amendment appeared, rewriting American history to legitimize the armed citizen unregulated except by his own ability to buy a gun at whatever price he could afford. The individual right to self-defense became conflated with the right to own a gun. In a dramatic move, an August 1977 article on the Second Amendment simply declared the gun owner as a private member of a general militia. "The guardians of our basic liberties are not formal bodies of police or military. They are not mercenaries hired to preserve and defend the rights of free men and women. The guardians of civil liberty are those, each individual, who would enjoy that liberty."[31] Forget the compromises of those turbulent postrevolutionary years that insisted on a militia that was "well-regulated" with officers and a chain of command, a hedge against abuse by either state or federal actions. Forget the intervening years of militia riots, disciplinary actions, and federal control. There would no longer be a chain of command through which civil, representative government might check excess. Now, Everyman was a militia island unto himself.

In 1979, Harlon Carter declared that the NRA was "foremost in the struggle to protect and preserve all our God-given, constitutional and long-accepted rights." He and the NRA were waging a "great battle. Strong men will not shirk or flinch. Free men cannot do so. Ours is a great revolution, which began on this continent 200 years ago."[32] Further, the mission of the NRA was "not the light-hearted pursuit of a sport, though there's nothing wrong with that." A new morality and political strategy formed in the late 1970s to counter perfectly the freedom marches, bus rides, sit-ins, and public demonstrations of dissent against government policy and white racism. The NRA had morphed again, becoming a "deep and serious voice of a people determined to be free."[33]

A select group of white men who savored conservative politics claimed the high moral ground of "the people." They likened themselves to the militia of old, defending liberty, but without any regulation, training, or officers. They claimed to be the heart of patriotic America. And they were armed and ready.

6

UNCIVIL RIGHTS

As I settled into a chair across from Frank in his tidy book-lined office, he quickly moved my cup of tea onto a piece of paper.[1] He explained that the desk was old and he didn't want any stains. He was good-natured and alert, with a can-do spirit running through his words. I couldn't detect the slightest hint of the deadly serious tone of gun advocates I'd listened to over the previous four years. Quite the opposite: he wanted to talk and reminisce about the old days. To Frank, there really wasn't any mystery at all about what had happened.

Why gun rights had became a political rallying cry was absolutely clear to him. It all started in the 1970s, but it came out of the energizing failures of the 1960s. Frank had been active in the Young Americans for Freedom and supported Barry Goldwater in his unsuccessful bid for the presidency against Lyndon

Johnson in 1964. The Young Americans for Freedom had started in 1960 with a meeting of young conservatives at the family home of William F. Buckley, Jr. in Sharon, Connecticut. Disenchanted with the policies of liberal Republicans and what they saw as a drift to the left in American politics, they composed the Sharon Statement, which became their guiding mandate.[2] Political freedom was equated with economic freedom, which was equated with the market economy. And international Communism was singled out as the "greatest single threat to these liberties."[3]

As a consequence, even President Eisenhower's containment policy against Communism was condemned in favor of the need to confront and destroy Communism globally through military means if necessary. Hawks with strong laissez-faire beliefs in capitalism, the Young Americans for Freedom set out to turn the Republican Party away from its strategy of consensus politics and toward their conservative positions. Recently, historians have examined how conservative grassroots groups like the Young Americans for Freedom organized on and off college campuses in the 1960s and '70s have effected significant changes in American politics, resulting in the 1980 election of Ronald Reagan, a longtime supporter of the group.[4]

Frank told me that in the early '70s, the Young Americans for Freedom had started a Student's Committee for the Right to Keep and Bear Arms.[5] That group transformed into a Second Amendment organization that other educational and lobbying groups imitated, fusing gun rights and conservative political causes. Soon afterward, in 1975, the National Rifle Association started its own lobbying arm, the Institute for Legislative Action, the most effective political lobby today. And more adamant groups formed, such as the Gun Owners of America, whose members reveled in far-right confrontation and keeping the heat on those gun-rights groups too willing to compromise their conservative beliefs.[6]

Frank laughed about those days, especially the internal squabbling within the NRA. In the 1970s, he said, "Bill Loeb thought the NRA had its head in the sand about the need for a gun lobby."[7] That was the first time I'd heard Bill Loeb's name associated with the gun lobby.

After that talk with Frank, I dove into the *American Rifleman* of the 1970s to follow this internal conflict. But before this interview in 2004, for me Loeb had always been the cantankerous, conservative voice of New Hampshire, the hard-hitting editor, pounding politicians, academics, and labor activists with his sharp tongue and far-right beliefs.

I can still recall the newspaper image of Edmund Muskie standing in front of the offices of Loeb's newspaper. Muskie was running for the Democratic nomination for president in 1972 and looked like he would win until that fateful day. Taking the editor to task for describing his wife as a drunk, Muskie railed against Loeb. Some reporters even claimed that he cried, which was the fatal blow. Whatever the truth, Muskie was finished as the Democratic candidate to run against Richard Nixon. He was labeled a "sissy." Even Nixon was amused. He knew he could beat George McGovern from South Dakota with his arms tied behind his back.[8]

Loeb hated the antics of people on the left.[9] And he hated anyone in the state of New Hampshire who provided a forum for views unlike his own, especially University of New Hampshire faculty who invited controversial speakers onto their campus or into their classrooms. His was the language of enemies and nasty political labeling. A take-no-prisoners brand of politics. Loeb provoked the NRA leadership to politicize the debate over guns in the United States.

Like Loeb, Frank was there at the start when the gun-rights movement caught fire as a conservative political force. Frank helped to organize educational and policy groups that quickly morphed into legislative lobbying forces. The relevance to campaign tactics was crystal-clear to him. The gun issue helped to elect Ronald Reagan and George W. Bush. People cast their ballots to protect what they perceived as threats to their guns. They perceived that liberals wanted their guns. Hence, they voted Republican. Frank seized on the hot issue, which was fueled by an emotional brew of anger, resentment, defiance, and fear.

In the 1970s, the Republican Party, like the NRA, was undergoing change. At the time, the Republicans were divided into two main camps: fiscal conservatives with moderate social positions, and ultraconservatives, many of whom had been Southern Democrats before their former party made common cause with the civil-rights movement. Politicians like Senator Strom Thurmond from South Carolina, who in 1956 drafted the "Southern Manifesto on Integration" in response to the Supreme Court decision of *Brown v. Board of Education*, became a familiar face in conservative publications like *The New Guard: The Magazine of Young Americans for Freedom*.[10] The political ground was shifting. The Republican Party gradually hardened its stance against progressive social causes and swung behind conservative political rhetoric—what was called "individual responsibility"—that effectively rid white Americans of social responsibility for the economic system from which they benefited.

But as I talked with Frank, I still didn't get it. Why guns? Weren't there other ways to rejuvenate the William Loeb brand of politics and the conservative political agenda?

His answer was quick. That one was easy. In the early 1970s, it was essential to "reverse the flow in the pipes." The language of civil rights needed a dramatic counter-force, a rhetorical push in the opposite direction. Frank had likened the civil-rights movement to a flood of water coursing through the veins of America's political plumbing, a flood starting in the 1960s with no end in sight. Lyndon Johnson had won big at the ballot box in 1964 with his political vision of the "Great Society." And the Democrats seemed invincible. The language of rights needed a massive redirection. And guns seemed to fit the emotional bill.

I agreed with Frank on one thing. To me and my friends during the 1960s, the language of civil rights had indeed stirred our political and moral imaginations. I could still hear President Johnson's Texas drawl when he said, "We shall overcome" in 1965, repeating the words of Martin Luther King, Jr. and the African American hymn that was carried by South Carolina tobacco workers into civil-rights groups. The United States did indeed seem capable of change when a white Southern Democrat could learn from a black leader and advocate for social and economic justice. The Voting Rights Act of 1965 did seem to change America into a place where the vote was guaranteed for every citizen, white, black, brown, rich, or poor. President Johnson seemed to speak directly to Southern blacks, denied the ballot in their home states by poll taxes, deceptive registration, and physical intimidation despite what the Fifteenth Amendment had told them in 1870.

And many Americans were listening when President Johnson presented his challenge. "This great, rich, restless country can offer opportunity and hope to all, all black and white, all North and South, sharecropper and city dweller. These are the enemies: poverty, ignorance, disease. They're our enemies, not our fellow man, not our neighbor. And these enemies too—poverty, disease, and ignorance: we shall overcome."[11]

But between 1965 and the early 1970s, these hopes had

crashed against a set of domestic barriers. They broke against
the harsh realities of local and state obstacles to fair housing, of
inflated rents, job barriers, and a war with Vietnam that would
cost America billions.[12] Gains were substantial, but often too
little, too late. Four months after Johnson preached hope, the
Watts riots exploded. Other cities followed suit: in 1967, the list
was long; Detroit, Chicago, Baltimore, and Atlanta faced the
burning of their inner-city neighborhoods. Homes and stores
were destroyed. My uncle saw his small luggage shop in Chicago
damaged by vandals. Faced with this and other economic ills,
he became a sullen and bitter man.

One year later, the country was overwhelmed by assassinations, massive nonviolent demonstrations, Yippies, Weather-
men, Black Panthers, and police brutality.[13] Yet despite this
significant internal turmoil, the assassinations of 1968 had created enough common ground for the Democrats and Republicans in Congress to pass the bipartisan Gun Control Act of
1968. Even President Nixon, never a favorite of the conservatives, had supported its passage. As a young aide to a politician,
Frank read batches of letters from disgruntled voters who hated
the Gun Control Act. The gun issue was hot—politically hot.
Despite bipartisan support for gun control, the Democrats were
perceived as more willing to support restrictions. Despite the
rumors that the NRA had a hand in the legislation, liberals were
targeted. The letters were angry. Emotions about guns ran high,
mixed with white paranoia and distrust of a government too
willing to listen to minorities and too permissive in beating back
political dissent.

Conservatives needed a movement to push against the Democratic party gains associated with civil rights. It was all how
you framed it, Frank explained. He was brilliant at framing it.
You couldn't say you were "pro-gun." That sounded bad. But you

could proudly say you were for "gun rights." All that was left was to model the gun-rights movement on the moral and political language of civil-rights activists and the effective organizational methods of the Young American for Freedom. Fears of gun registration and handgun confiscation united certain Americans. Their gun votes for specific politicians on both the state and national level helped to "reverse the flow." Gun rights checked civil rights.

From my reading, I knew that in 1971, the *New Guard* had run an article called "An Aspect of Freedom: The Right to Bear Arms."[14] Written by John M. Snyder, the article framed the conflict over gun laws with a short summary of the Constitution and the Bill of Rights, especially the Second Amendment. Individual ownership of weapons became the foundation of "freedom," and as a result conveniently countered the collective nonviolent political language of civil rights. The controversial post–Civil War amendments to the Constitution, extending political rights to disenfranchised minorities and women, were silenced. Instead, the loud drumbeat of the Second Amendment drowned out the rhetoric of civil rights fought for so hard and long by women and minorities who wanted access to political and economic power.

Individualism, not collective action, and ownership, not partnership in the political process, redefined the language of rights by ambitious conservatives like Ronald Reagan, Jesse Helms, George F. Will, Barry Goldwater, and Phyllis Schlafly. Snyder's short discussion of the Second Amendment preceded a refocusing on his main rationale for gun ownership: to stop crime. And crime statistics were trotted out to prove that restrictions on gun sales and ownership did not reduce crime. More interesting than the use of statistics to refute restrictions on guns was the linkage of individualism, private ownership, and crime prevention to promote a conservative set of political beliefs. The social need to address the historic and systemic problems of racial and gender discrimination, labor conflict, and poverty was eliminated. Civil rights became civil riots.

Attempts to address "crime and disorder" through any restrictions on firearms was labeled "utopian and statist." Armed individuals were a key line of defense against crime, along with more effective law enforcement and mandatory minimum penalties. Issues of social and economic justice were reduced to a mere sentence: "Where poverty and alienation are found to constitute an environment for those socially destructive tendencies which so often result in criminal activity, they could possibly be reduced."[15] But the agency to reduce crime became the individual, armed and ready to protect his place of business and his home. Individual power was glorified through the heroics of self-defense. Politics became deeply personal, embedded in the private emotional space of self-protection.

In an impassioned plea, Snyder asked for a "democratic" answer to gun laws. "It rests on faith in the people. It does not evidence fear of people possessing firearms as does the statist approach. The democratic approach is not found embodied in the writings of the super statists, the totalitarians, people like V. I. Lenin, who called for 'the disarming of the bourgeoisie.'"[16] This version of power to the people via gun ownership resonates well within the pages of the *New Guard*, a magazine that vilified most progressive social movements in the 1960s and '70s as tinged with Communism and the liberal virus. Owning guns became the linchpin of a new political theory. To stand up and lift your Winchester rifle above your head was equivalent to the black power salute. Conservative whites now had their rallying cry of rights to wave in front of the nation.

But a single article in the *New Guard* could not in itself shift the political landscape. It would take people like Frank years to shape these raw emotions into a political force that could reverse the flow in the pipes. First, Frank needed to build the membership for the "gun rights" movement. In the early years, Frank used the lists from gun magazines and other military or mercenary publications like *Soldier of Fortune*.[17] Returning Vietnam vets in the 1970s were another potential pool. War veterans didn't want "to be told that they couldn't use certain guns." The demographic was blue-collar. Frank reminded me that the old NRA, prior to the 1970s, had catered to the wealthy with their sporting clubs and the white middle-class with recreational hunting and target shooting. The new NRA would cross class lines to the blue-collar crowd. Gun-control advocates could easily be painted as "elitist" in this new politics. They were the typical liberals telling you what was good for you. They knew better. They always insisted they were morally superior. Some people were fed up.

There were many different reasons that people in the United States wanted forms of gun control. Frank said it was too complicated. He needed to make it simple and direct. It was all about perception. "Gun-grabber." He loved the term. I've read it hundreds of times in gun-lobby magazines and advertisements. Frank was right. It was all about perception.

Frank enjoyed looking back. He was animated and confident. I forgot about my tea getting colder on his desk as he enumerated the reasons people were against guns. There were the "animal people," the group who hated hunting. There was the "nonviolent" crowd, pacifists who in principle were against killing. There were the urbanites that were worried about crime. They wanted to keep guns off the streets. And then there was that last group, people who don't own guns and don't like guns. They don't even want to touch them.

Keep it simple. "Gun-grabbers" worked much better. "Put everyone in one category." Frank thought it was cutting-edge. He helped frame the issues for the movement.

From his perspective, the movement was successful and gaining ground every day. The future of gun rights was very "bright," despite the fact that membership has slumped under George W. Bush, when the threats have been perceived as few. Membership peaked under Bill Clinton.

Frank was proud of his political victories: he felt he was a "force" in getting votes for Reagan from the Democrats. He direct-mailed gun owners and used a targeted campaign strategy. The blue-collar folks switched parties. The gains of the Democrats during the civil-rights era, which produced the landslide victory of Lyndon Johnson in 1964, were effectively over. He didn't want to talk about Richard Nixon much; after all, he was the president who enforced the Gun Control Act, and he was suspected of secretly wanting severe gun control. But the gun-rights movement paid off for Reagan, and even more so for George W. Bush. He was convinced that Al Gore "lost in Tennessee because of the gun issue," and that Gore's losses in West Virginia and Arkansas had the gun-rights movement to blame.

I had heard this same opinion expressed by the leaders of the NRA at their 2002 annual convention in Reno. Several wanted George W. Bush to come and personally thank them for their support. He didn't.

My time for this interview was up way too fast. Frank insisted that I take home with me a stack of books and journals on the Second Amendment movement. Historians, legal scholars, and policy makers were writing impassioned essays on how to protect our American gun rights. In fact, gun rights were a basic human right, a universal issue.

Before I left for another interview, Frank had a few words of caution. He told me that he worried about the "boiling point." To him, the gun-rights movement was a protection against massive civil unrest. If Congress passed a law to ban all handguns, America would blow. Citizens from across the country would rise up against the tyrants. This "Second American Revolution" would scald the country. Society would rip apart. If people are threatened, you don't know what they will do, he reminded me. America needed the gun-rights movement to keep that from happening.

I tried to remember what it was like to live through the 1960s and early '70s. The two words "boiling point" brought back memories. Oddly enough, I had started out in high school supportive of Barry Goldwater's run for president and critical of John F. Kennedy. A product of parochial schools and the Polish American community, I learned to mimic the anti-Communist mantra at the drop of a hat. My moral categories were simple, and I learned racial fear early. I knew exactly when to get off the subway in Chicago and could fret about the threat from the inner city, even though my father laughed at the paranoia of white Americans. I was a transition kid from the Polish neighborhoods to the white suburbs. (The big scandal while living in Skokie happened when a Jewish couple tried to sell a home to a black family; everyone was up in arms.) But going to college in the 1960s had given me hope instead of fear. Like many of my peers, I was swept up in the civil-rights and antiwar movements and worked, as they and I still do, for a society open and responsive to its citizens. I looked on in dismay as the Young

Americans for Freedom demonstrated against people like César Chávez and called community activists engaged in peaceful reform "bomb throwers" and "Communists." Crime was a label used by conservatives to discredit many effective private and public programs that confronted poverty, discrimination, and even hunger. Reading articles in the the *New Guard* debunking federal programs like the Office of Economic Opportunity (OEO) and redefining poverty as an affliction of individuals who didn't have the energy or desire to work, I realized how effective these tactics were. They made criminals not only of liquor-store robbers, but also of men and women who worked for a more just society, casting them as radicals working for violent global revolution.[18] The power-to-the people language of many social activists ran straight into the bootstrap language of the conservatives who criminalized dissent. The gun-rights movement seemed to come from the guts of people who believed social change was dangerous, even catastrophic. Where I felt hope, they experienced only threat.

A number of people that I interviewed told me that they began to use a gun for personal protection after the Watts riots in 1965. They didn't live in Los Angeles or even in California, but the country didn't feel safe anymore. One man who had grown up on a ranch in Colorado was clear about his reaction. And it really wasn't about owning guns at all. Where he lived, "guns were everywhere." Twenty-two-caliber rifles were "pest control." Every season, he hunted with his brothers. "Handguns were ubiquitous." But they never showed up at school or a dance. There was "no human violence."

After Watts, he changed his perception of America. A "rule of lawlessness" roamed the land. The riots "motivated" him to buy his first handgun for personal protection. Drafted into the army, he had to move to Baltimore for training. But in the city, it was unlawful to carry a firearm in the car or on your person. He felt strongly that he needed protection. "Instead of carrying a handgun in the car, I carried an entrenching tool." Standard issue for the army, the folding shovel was an "effective weapon," especially when carefully sharpened. He also carried a fire extinguisher. They "were of comfort" to him.

Nothing ever happened. He remembered blacks sitting on urban stoops. "There was anger in the streets." He felt uneasy; people were "glaring" at him. He admitted that the "media was important in polarizing" him. Dangers lurked in every corner. He reminded me that today in the United States there are "Two hundred and forty million guns in sixty million households." Their "use is small." But he felt he needed weapons for personal protection in the new America of the late 1960s—what several men I have interviewed called their "insurance policy." You wouldn't leave home without your credit card, your cell phone, or even your AAA membership. The gun was like that.

The boiling point spilled over into white America in other ways. Despite President Johnson's plea to reach all Americans, some felt "betrayed." The demands for economic democracy by black leaders like Whitney M. Young, Jr. of the National Urban League meant that the unions in America would have to change. Growing up in the white ethnic communities of Chicago, I knew two things about the city. Immigrants from Southern and Eastern Europe had the Catholic Church and the unions to ease the transition to their new country. Blacks migrating in from the South had neither. They lived in a vital, religious world parallel to mine and often had to fight the local union for jobs.

To working-class whites, blacks had been used to bust unions. They were strikebreakers. There were exceptions, of course. Young wrote in 1969 that "quite a few unions" joined the civil-rights movement. They "recruit black workers" and "carry out social projects of great importance, often in the face of opposition from bigoted members."[19] And the fact that Martin Luther King, Jr. was assassinated in the midst of the Memphis sanitation strike demonstrates how the civil-rights movement overlapped with a broader-based workers' movement challenging both state and business interests.[20] The 1968 election had shown the racist, political face of many union members. White auto workers went to the polls for George Wallace, despite the fact that members of the United Auto Workers Union and others fought for workers, whether white or black.[21]

By 1974, the Young Americans for Freedom had the slogans down pat. Gun rights were a bumper-sticker issue. You could pick your slogan and order as many stickers as you wanted through the *New Guard*: GUNS DON'T KILL PEOPLE, PEOPLE KILL PEOPLE; IF GUNS ARE OUTLAWED ONLY OUTLAWS WILL HAVE GUNS; SUPPORT YOUR RIGHT TO BEAR ARMS; CRIME CONTROL! NOT GUN CONTROL; GOON CONTROL NOT GUN CONTROL; REGISTER COMMUNISTS NOT FIREARMS. Thirty years later the slogans are the same, and the use of rights language to preach a conservative politics and morality is more firmly part of the American political fabric than ever.

In 2004, at the NRA annual convention, I stood next to a table of white-haired women handing out information on restaurants in Pittsburgh. They were listening to a white-haired man dressed in Bermuda shorts lecture them about his rights. How he had rights and the government was trying to take them away. How he had an inalienable right to his gun. How he would fight for this right, and that he voted. He was one of thousands of men at the convention who were fired up about their patriotic duty to defend the Second Amendment.

The conservatives in the Young Americans for Freedom who had supported Barry Goldwater, Ronald Reagan, Jesse Helms, and Strom Thurmond have fared well in the years since. The gun as a political fetish helped to catalyze the new politics of the conservatives and refocus the nation away from solving racial inequality, poverty, and social injustice. The conservative agenda to stop the Equal Rights Amendment, undermine unions, build up the military, and reframe social issues into crime-and-punishment mini-dramas found an emotional ally in the belief that gun ownership was necessary for freedom. A new era of uncivil rights had emerged in the United States.

PART THREE

7

RIDING THE REAGAN HIGHWAY

In the spring of 2004, I drove to Kankakee, Illinois, on U.S. 24, a road that is known in central Illinois as the Ronald Reagan Trail, passing through a string of emptied rural towns, each marked with a crowded green cemetery. It seemed as if the living had packed up and left generations of their deceased behind to speculate about the erased world of small-town America. Brilliant redbuds and dogwoods broke the monotony of crewcut lawns and spotless sidewalks, their scarlet flowers the only sharp cry against the loneliness of the streets. At their edges, flat brown cornfields dotted with aluminum silos stretched as far as the eye could see.

Ronald Reagan had grown up in several of these rural communities: Tampico, Dixon, Galesburg, and Eureka. Reflecting on his youth during the first year of his presidency in 1980, he felt that everything good that happened to him could be traced to his years on a small Christian campus in Eureka where he discovered his three loves: drama, politics, and sports.[1] And like many others born and raised in these communities, Ronnie left to find his destiny elsewhere. Born in Tampico, Ronald Reagan had lived for a dozen years in neighboring Dixon. After graduating from Eureka College, he wandered in the Midwest for a few years as a radio sports announcer and then walked away from farming communities for good. Called "Dutch" by his friends, he quickly grafted onto his Illinois roots the persona of the Hollywood actor who could stroll easily from the movie set to the political stage. Like so many other Americans, he left his home community behind in the slowly dying economies of rural America, their future tucked away in sleepy rows of carefully tended graves. What Reagan did not leave behind, however, was the language of the heartland, the small-town talk of country and decent American values, a political language that would provide the social glue for a rejuvenated form of national identity intent on purging its soul of shame or the urgent need to change.

Taking the Reagan Trail to the Kankakee gun show made perfect sense. In 1980, Reagan was the only U.S. president up to that point to win the endorsement of the National Rifle Association. His run for the office in 1980 succeeded partly because of grassroots organizational tactics aimed at wooing disgruntled gun owners, in particular white working-class men who had turned away from the Democratic Party and labor unions to embrace the political language of gun rights advocated by the conservative wing of the Republican Party.[2]

In 1983, Reagan was made an NRA "honorary life member," and when he addressed the NRA Legislative Session, meeting in Phoenix, Arizona, he made a promise to the American people:

"We will never disarm any American who seeks to protect his or her family from fear and harm."[3] Reagan made it clear that he felt "a special bond with members of your group."[4] And he complimented the leadership of the post-1977 NRA, specifically Harlon Carter and the Institute for Legislative Action. He joked with his audience and echoed the familiar themes of the gun-rights movement. The people in the NRA were law-abiding, decent people. The problem was crime. "We have declared war on organized crime and the career criminal in America."[5] He talked about how hunters were conservationists and how his administration was guided by stewardship of the land.

In his speech, Reagan legitimized the gun as a political weapon. The "right" owners were law-abiders who fought with passion against the criminals who abused and threatened America. The "right" gun owners were crime fighters on the domestic front, protecting home and hearth. Likewise, as head of the nation, he was the "right" man for the fight against Communism. "The United States remains the last, best hope for a mankind plagued by tyranny and deprivation."[6] He would never back off from his promises to revitalize the military, protect El Salvador's democracy from Communist guerrillas, and make sure the prized gun of World War II veterans, the M1, could be purchased through the civilian marksmanship program, run at that point by the Department of Defense.[7]

Harlon Carter was pleased. "Yesterday, my friends, you saw for the first time in NRA history a sitting President of the United States stand with us and affirm the freedoms and affirm the good citizenship and affirm our Second Amendment rights, the things that we believe in and which we support."[8] The gun had worked its magic. The good citizens had returned to the public space of American politics, and they were armed.

During Reagan's tenure, a number of congressional leaders

worked to make the Second Amendment integral to how Americans thought about that magic word, freedom. In 1982, Orrin G. Hatch, as chairman of the Senate Subcommittee on the Constitution, under the Committee of the Judiciary, which was chaired by Strom Thurmond, insisted that his committee would "concern itself with a proper recognition of, and respect for, this right most valued by free men."[9] He saw his chance to reconnect the dots between "our ancestors" who "forged a land" conceived in liberty with their trusty "musket and rifle."[10]

Not surprisingly, during the 1980s, a new generation of male action heroes such as Arnold Schwarzenegger, Sylvester Stallone, and Chuck Norris burst onto the movie screen. These men, some armed to the teeth, were what the cultural critic Susan Jeffords has called the "hard bodies" of the new masculinity.[11] Others, like Charles Bronson in his maudlin *Death Wish* movies, were quiet men who overnight became enforcers of a vigilante pledge to confront the criminal and revenge the evils inflicted on family and home. The psychotic predator who roamed the streets of America, raping and killing white women, returned to haunt the dreams of law-abiding white male citizens. Faced with an ineffective police force and an apathetic society, these fictional quiet men took up guns and hunted down the rabble scum of the ghettoes and assorted poor neighborhoods that bred vermin, amoral freaks of nature worthy only of private execution. The psychic investment in guns paid off at the polls for Reagan and the gun-rights movement. The NRA was not the breeding ground of gun nuts. It was the fountain of freedom, legitimized in its politics by the President of the United States.[12]

In 1986, Reagan helped to pass the Firearms Owners' Protection Act (FOPA), which created a boom in gun shows throughout the United States. By making it easier for licensed dealers to sell away from their place of business, gun shows became much more than small-scale events for antique and historical gun collectors and their hunting buddies.[13] Under new federal regulations, gun-shows became big business for commercial gun dealers. As one major gun-show organizer put it, FOPA created an "entrepreneurial opportunity." A perfect Reagan-era formula for America: capitalism, consumerism, and conservative politics wrapped in the born-again language of rights for gun owners.

Cities like Reno, Houston, and Los Angeles would host enormous commercial gun markets. Domestic sales would continue to skyrocket, saturating handgun sales until they peaked in the early 1990s.[14] This gun-show boom would eventually account for 40 percent of all gun transfers in the United States.[15] Most of this buying frenzy had bypassed Kankakee. That is not to say that people in Kankakee don't own their fair share of the national investment in firearms. But in contrast to other high-profile gun shows, Kankakee's was a flea market, held in a county fairgrounds building filled with aging white men and clusters of veterans telling war stories, pushing gun rights, and testifying to their defiant struggle for freedom.

Rows of folding tables were spread with junk guns, old rifles and military surplus. There was a long set of tables covered with *Lord of the Rings* weapons, huge swords with names like Glamdring, Sting, Narsil, and Hadhafang, next to stacks of partially opened boxes of surplus fantasy guns. Other tables had piles of action novels, well-thumbed and worn, intermixed with a few sticky-sweet romances.

Most tables had a small yellow sign with the black letters F O I D printed on them. I quickly learned that this stood for Firearms Owner's Identification Card and was necessary because the people "up there" were crazy. "Up there" was the city of Chicago, all of which was presumed to be in league with the Illinois State Police, who had enforced a background check and photo ID requirement on all gun owners and purchasers in the state. Application forms were at the gun show, as were booths where people provided help on how to fill them out. Even though some men told me that the FOID reduced crime and domestic violence, the grousing about the FOID was rampant throughout the show. Illinois was doomed. "Only Illinois has such a system." When exhibitors found out I was from Washington State, they repeatedly told me, "Your state is free." The wild, open, free West still had that magical hold on their political imaginations. The state laws regulating gun ownership strictly measured freedom. More state regulation, less political freedom. Gun ownership was the litmus test for their democracy.

After the fourth conversation about my good fortune not to live in Illinois, I nodded politely and went to find a cup of coffee. Along the wall of the exhibition hall, two Vietnamese women sold cokes, hot dogs, and doughnuts at a concession stand. They spoke their clipped tonal language while handing out food. These two women were the only people of color I saw at the show. A handful of white women walked the aisles, but the place was filled with middle-aged and elderly white men. The contrast with the community outside was sharp. Kankakee's population was 47 percent white and 41 percent black, with the remaining 12 percent divided between Hispanics, Native Americans, and Asian Americans. As in the rest of the United States, the gun-rights movement and gun-show phenomenon have their base primarily in the actions and imaginations of white men.

I grabbed a sugar glazed and sat down at a table to organize my notes. Three men sitting two tables away talked intensely about their experiences in the 82nd Airborne. Across the aisle, guns advertised as semi-automatic M16s complete with extra magazines and ammo were stacked for sale. The protests about freedom blended with war stories and low-pitched sales of military weapons used in every major armed conflict of the twentieth century.

After my break, I spent some time at a booth talking with a guy selling historical guns. He was eager to show me a World War I bayonet. He let me hold it and told me I could buy a pre-1895 gun without an FOID. He then started telling me about Chicago and how bad it was "up there." How they were always rioting up there. They riot for anything. They riot if it's hot outside. He was thankful that they weren't rioting as much any more. He talked as if the 1968 violence in the inner city had happened yesterday. On the day that Martin Luther King, Jr. spoke with passion about economic injustice and a renewed commitment to nonviolence and was gunned down in Memphis, the inner-city neighborhoods of Chicago exploded. This man saw the flames of the ghetto as senseless criminal actions devoid of reason.

Like Reagan, the man selling historical military guns looked back on the 1960s as a time of crisis when American values went into a downward spiral. When Robert F. Kennedy was assassinated in 1968 two months after King, Reagan wrote a letter to his teenage daughter, Patti, and said: "Now is one of those moments when I'm grateful that I can be in a position to perhaps change things to see that we do start a return to sanity and law and order and turn away from this whole creed of violence that seems to be so prevalent in our land."[16] One result of the political assassinations of King and RFK was the 1968 Gun Control Act, an act that Reagan helped to revise in 1986 to protect gun owners.

For Ronald Reagan, the way of the gun was the road to freedom. Gun running was at the heart of the Reagan years.[17] In places like Central America, Cambodia, and Angola—without large-scale industries to produce guns—the military was heavily armed partly because of the Reagan-era gun-running operations. The legacy of this small arms race is today felt acutely across the globe.[18]

The Kankakee gun show was awash in freedom stories. There were 120 years' worth of tales in the guns laid across the tables. A man in his nineties told me that both his grandfathers had used Springfield rifles in the Spanish American War. He was proud to be selling an 1884 Springfield. He pointed out how the beautiful wooden rifle stock had been authenticated. These rifles were his family history.

At the Veterans of Foreign Wars booth, a World War II vet talked fast about how many friends he lost in the war. He liked to go to schools and talk about history: How Truman didn't know what kind of weapon the A-bomb was; how the A-bomb saved American lives, and how the politicians didn't let the soldiers in Vietnam win that war. The vet sitting next to him selling raffle tickets who had been stationed in Thailand during Vietnam didn't say a word. He sat there staring in silence.

The hands of the World War II vet fluttered as he handed me the local VFW calendar of events. The April calendar reported that there were "not many members at our post meetings." The solution was to "let all members know we meet the last Thursday each month." They had more than 200 members in the local VFW post. Their slogan was: "We'd do anything for this country."

I listened to these stories knowing that a high percentage of men lie about their years in the military. Books have been written documenting these deceptions. I have walked gun shows with vet friends who remind me that men love to lie about war.

Tread carefully. Everyone wants to return from war a hero to wash away the blood with public celebration or to gain respect for a support job spent in boredom miles from action. What kind of stories are there for the six to twelve men or women needed to back up the one soldier in the field? How to spice up the filing job or electronic monitoring with the smell of sweat and sacrifice?

The vets sold and traded their weapons and repeated the past in familiar tales. What the VFW vet told me echoed what I had heard in Reagan's speeches throughout the 1980s, particularly the charged history of our wars. Americans should stand up and be proud. Americans are free of blame for dropping the A-bomb. Americans are free of blame for losing the war in Vietnam. Americans must unite behind a strong defense, the right to arm the individual, the need to arm the police, the urgency to strengthen the military, the rightness of arming freedom fighters throughout the globe. These stories freed us as a country from sin and failure. They absolved us of our past. And they legitimized our unique and necessary future—to ensure democracy in the globe with a stockpile of weapons to get the job done. They made war—with its butcheries and irrationality—acceptable. They reassured us even in the face of the complexities of geopolitics, economic injustice, and global instability.

Before I left the VFW booth, the World War II vet told me that he had Gandhi on his list of the ten most important people in the world. But there are "some things you have to do." He had a dream that there would be a future where no VFWs would need to exist; in the meantime he believed in gun rights.[19] But it was Reagan, not Gandhi, who dominated the stories of the Kankakee gun show.

At the NRA annual convention in Reno, Nevada, two years before my trip to Kankakee, I had watched a video narrated by

Charlton Heston about Reagan and his 658-acre "Western White House," Rancho del Cielo, in the Santa Ynez Mountains of Southern California. As Heston strolled the empty ranch, pointing out where Ronnie kept his guns and chopped wood, the crowd of 5,000 at the annual members meeting sat in reverential silence. A few minutes of video bliss created a direct line between the gun-rights movement and the U.S. presidency. Ronnie was still on their side. Even though Reagan was not in the video, he was presented through voice-overs and Heston's comments as the ever-faithful president, standing between them and the disarmament of the American people, ever ready to defend their role as freedom fighters.

When I left the gun show and walked outside, the prairie wind was swelling. I could hear the horses whinnying in the neighboring pastures. I stood out in the parking lot, waiting for my ride. A man in his seventies stopped his car, leaned over the passenger seat, and asked how I liked the show. "Okay," I responded.

He searched around on the car floor and said he wanted to show me a pistol from the French Indochina War that he owned. He had special bullets made for it, refitted .32s. Pretty expensive. But he liked to shoot the gun. There was a U.S. Marine Corps baseball cap on the passenger seat. He wanted me to know that the French Indochina War happened before we went into Vietnam. Same place. Same type of war.

He smiled at me when he drove away.

I stood there wondering what another Midwesterner born thirty-three years before Reagan under similar modest circumstances in central Illinois would say about my experience of riding the Reagan Highway. Carl Sandburg, one of America's most popular poets, who went to the Spanish American War as a young man and made it back to later witness and write about the 1919 race riots in Chicago, was passionate about the need to create a civil society that confronted labor conflict, racial inequalities, and greed.[20] The gun had no answers in the hands of either the state or the citizens. But the answers were there if one stopped and listened.

For the young Sandburg, democracy was in the soil of the prairies. The obstacle to democracy was found in the hearts and minds of people who resisted its truth and necessary sacrifices. Society could sustain communities and institutions intent on both justice and freedom, but not without a collective belief in its possibility. Human security was the work of everyone. Now, Sandburg's voice was silenced on this prairie. Instead, the Kankakee gun show asked citizens to undergo the political litmus test of the gun.

8

DETERRENTS

The stuffed elk and deer heads on the walls in Peter's den were oblivious to our conversation. Even the large river otter frozen on the table covered with books and *Commentary* magazines looked away. I wanted to think they were witnesses; that our talk of guns and crime would hold their interest, that the deer head over the computer, flanked by turkey feathers and rigid geese, would nod in agreement or roll its Bambi eyes in dissent. Instead the animals were immobile, covered in a thin layer of dust and dog hair, immune to our conversation about crime.

An economist close to retirement, Peter told me that I had to understand crime.[1] If I understood crime and criminal behavior, I would understand why guns were a fundamental right for Americans. I thought back on how conservatives in the

1970s had made crime the center of how Americans thought about their cities, towns, and neighborhoods, and how Reagan promised never to disarm Americans in their fight to defend their homes. With the help of TV, movies, newspapers, radio, and politicians, crime was like a gigantic filter through which many Americans looked at their country's social, economic, and political conflicts. Crime was the beast roaming within the nation's walls.

Peter also insisted that I had to understand choice. Choice was the essence of economics. Choice was the essence of crime. I had to think about crime in terms of costs and benefits. Benefits are "what you get." Costs are "what you lose." I felt like I was being drilled in basic economics. And I was.

My conversation three years ago with Peter about gun rights has stayed with me past the usual erosions of time. His words have since been echoed in many other conversations with gun advocates who belong to no lunatic fringe but insist on the clarity of their thought and the inevitability of its application. They are the educated, rational gun owners who read, think, and follow the logic that guns are deterrents.

Peter, with his advanced degrees and intellectual intensity, was part of a sober crew who thought about guns through the lens of geopolitical tactics. Political arguments about the militia and the Second Amendment were of little interest to him. The FBI and their firepower were concerns, but the tyranny of the state was not a major problem. Peter insisted that I had to understand that the major problem was personal security. Gun control was a "pacifist movement." "You cannot ensure that others will give up their gun." The unarmed citizen had no deterrents. He wanted me to remember MAD. Mutual Assured Destruction. That strategy had worked during the Cold War. Its opposite, unilateral disarmament, was wrong. Deterrents were the best way to control negative human behavior. "It takes two to have peace, and one to have war." If a criminal knows you have a gun, he will not attack.

The word "deterrent" is worth pausing over. Coming from the root *de-terrer*, it means to frighten, or turn aside by fear. The word "terrorist" shares the same linguistic origin. Deterrents work through both real and perceived threats. I can frighten you only if you believe or know that I have the ability to create the fear's possible consequence: harm, or even death. And worse, my fear of you, the reason I need a deterrent to provoke a counter-fear, might rest on a maze of anxieties and ignorance. I may not know you at all or have the faintest clue of how to deter you effectively. My deterrent might be worse than my perceived enemy. This is heady stuff, the meat of espionage and deception.

The analogy with the Cold War and thermonuclear weapons has become a favorite with Peter and other gun-rights advocates. John Lott, the intellectual authority behind much that I hear in these gun-rights arguments, also used this analogy. "If outlawing guns would primarily affect their ownership by law-abiding citizens, this research indicates that at least in the short run, we would expect crime rates to rise. The discussion is very similar to the debate over nuclear disarmament. A world without nuclear weapons might be better off, but unilateral disarmament may not be the best way to accomplish that goal."[2] An economist like Peter, Lott wrote the influential *More Guns, Less Crime* and has been defending his position with statistics ever since.

According to this way of thinking, citizens, along with their enemies, the criminals, are likened to nation-states armed with weapons of mass destruction. The question of whether to ban guns altogether breaks down because of the impossibility of "unilateral disarmament." Criminals would find a way to hold on to their weapons, and at the very least, crime rates would probably increase and the transition to a gun-free society take too long. Instead, to prevent crime, private citizens must own guns. A microcosm of the Cold War arms race is played out in American households. Indeed, such self-defense principles resonate with the Cold War logic of MAD, the brainchild of Herman Kahn, who developed the concept when he was a RAND analyst, working on U.S. military strategy in the 1950s.[3]

Deterrence has become a powerful concept in justifying why Americans need gun rights.[4] The defense intellectuals like Kahn who helped shape military tactics and strategy during the Cold War have their counterparts in self-defense intellectuals who promoted strategies about protecting hearth and home. Deterrents are a hot topic for theorists and propagandists who pile on statistics to prove that gun ownership by citizens significantly reduces crime rates. In *Guns, Crime, and Freedom*, Wayne LaPierre, the executive director of the NRA, writes that the individual armed citizen is "the best deterrent to violent criminal attack," and he backs his position up with research from criminologists.[5]

Opponents to this position fought back, mounting their own evidence from criminologists, that produce the opposite results. The Violence Policy Center and the Brady Center to Prevent Gun Violence publish and post on their web sites statistics on how handguns in particular do not deter crime and might even escalate crime. The battle over whether private firepower works to bust crime has become as passionate as the debates over nuclear weapons to stop Communism in its tracks were back in the 1950s.

Ironically, under the shadow of thermonuclear war, the armed citizen in the 1950s stepped forward as a gun owner with a renewed mission of civil defense. Hints of this shift are seen in definitions of the gun owner as a guerrilla fighter, standing his ground in the chaotic landscape of these terrifying "new weapons of war." A 1958 editorial in the *American Rifleman* described how living with nuclear and guided missiles made it clear that "the individual soldier and the individual citizen will be forced to rely upon the weapon with which he is armed and on his own ability to use it effectively, if he is to survive."[6] Who would defend average Americans against the waves of anarchy and social chaos when the bomb strikes? The government's preparedness for civil defense was a joke to some gun owners. But when civilian gun owners organized on their own to form "an American 'underground' to oppose any potential enemy with guerrilla tactics," they were quickly reminded by a sharp editorial in the *American Rifleman* that "non-military civil defense capability at the state and local level must be developed within the framework of existing governments."[7]

Patriotic gun owners could join government-regulated groups under command to fight if and when the bomb dropped, but as citizens they had no formal role, except in their own homes. There they might think of themselves as civil-defense guerrilla fighters, protecting the homestead against the marauding hordes certain to come. In what they saw as an increasingly brutal and decadent America, they could stand their ground. These Cold War emotions sharpened the distinction between a patriot and a criminal. Deterrents were as important to keep the Soviet Union in check as they were against the threatening burglar. Deterrents would stop criminals from invading the home.

Recently, both the Centers for Disease Control and Prevention and the National Academy of Sciences have entered the fray about whether guns in private hands act as deterrents to crime. The evidence on both sides of the debate has not convinced either organization that guns or gun control either reduce or increase crime. Far more work needs to be done before we can claim with certainty that guns in the hands of a citizen were indeed effective deterrents, or that gun control, taking these deterrents out of the hands of private citizens, lessened crime.[8]

But these endless arguments over statistics didn't seem to get at the heart of what I was hearing from Peter and his intellectual peers. They seemed more like props in a conflict with deep roots in the pit of our society. After all, Peter assured me that it all came down to human behavior. Criminals were rational and would not attack someone who had a gun, but a gun as a deterrent was about instilling fear and frightening someone away or stopping him dead in his tracks. And fear takes us on a long journey through the world of everyday anxieties about how we know our world. On the simplest level, I had to ask Peter how the criminal would know I had a gun. Deterrents needed some measure of credibility and certainty, or why have all those billions going into intelligence systems and satellites? Maybe I had watched too many Cold War spy movies.

Peter reassured me that the criminal would only have to look through his windows and see all the trophy heads and know he had guns in the house. He added, "You don't observe the deterrent's effects." Crimes simply do not happen as frequently to people with guns. He told me to read John Lott carefully because his book had proven this point. Criminals interviewed in prison confirmed that they would not burglarize a home with guns in it. They didn't want to face the consequences.

That made sense to me. If I was a burglar sitting in a prison cell and was asked if I would rob a house with an armed and ready owner inside, I would definitely say no. But how did they know the homes had guns? Was it common knowledge in the neighborhood of the criminal? Was there a little decal on the front door stating that there was a gun inside? Or were there guns hung in plain sight above the fireplace or on the wall for criminals to see when they peered into the windows?

As in the Cold War, knowing what weapons the enemy had was critical to the strategy of deterrents. And knowledge about the enemy's military capabilities was frequently distorted to garnish power and justify funding.[9] Further, deterrents functioned in a complex world of visible and invisible weapons; stockpiles camouflaged in the desert, hidden in mountain caves, and roaming on railroad cars. Deceptive and real claims and counterclaims could and did escalate an "arms race" or perhaps even cause a war. How could I apply Peter's language about the Cold War to home defense?

These were not idle questions. At gun shows, I am often encouraged to buy a particular gun because it can be concealed. The stock of a gun always gives it away, the dealer will insist. Best to buy a gun that can be invisible in your holster attached at your lower back or in your specially built purse or fanny pack. Making a gun visible, what is called brandishing a weapon, was a hot topic for gun owners, between whom there is much disagreement over what type of tactics to use if and when you are assaulted.

John Lott has been roundly criticized for reporting on how often a crime was stopped by someone brandishing a weapon. Early in his book *More Guns, Less Crime*, he claimed that in a national survey he administered, "98 percent of the time that people use guns defensively, they merely have to brandish a weapon to break off an attack."[10] Day after day, law-abiding citizens simply pulled out their guns and showed them. "Brandishing," like "deterrent," was a potent word, coming from the strong Teutonic root, *brand*, or sword. It didn't take much imagination to visualize a knight or highway robber waving around a nasty metal blade—a medieval deterrent, or a crime sword. But in the modern world, guns were regulated in the United States, and we don't walk down Main Street with our sidearms strapped to our hips. Brandishing a weapon to threaten or intimidate brings us to the murky world of human gestures and threats.

I've heard and read many brandishing stories over the last few years. One retired military officer I interviewed was upset that brandishing was even considered a deterrent. If you show your gun, you must be willing to fire it, he told me. He hated all the stories about how people stopped crime by merely waving a pistol. Still other stories claimed that the mere gesture of reaching to show a gun had saved a person's life. Chased in a road-rage incident, one man simply gestured to the floor of his car as if he were going for his gun, and the bad guys veered away. He didn't even own a gun. I couldn't help thinking that if I was being chased by a truck and I stooped to pick up something on my car's floor, the guys following me would assume I had dropped my lipstick or comb. Gestures, especially in a situation of threat or danger, have multiple meanings with outcomes dependent upon a world of cultural knowledge about men, women, and who wields power.

But Peter was convinced that the gun in the hands of a private citizen was a foolproof deterrent. I was hung up on the guessing game, the "Russian Roulette" strategy of carrying concealed weapons as a crime-busting technique. I have since found out that John Lott had answers to some of my questions. According to Lott, the criminal did not know specifically that the potential victim had a gun, and that was okay. In fact, because handguns were concealed, the criminal must risk confrontation with a potentially armed citizen whenever he or she attempted to commit a crime. Risky business, indeed. Further, he wrote that "citizens who have no intention of ever carrying concealed handguns in a sense get a 'free ride' from the crime-fighting efforts of their fellow citizens."[11]

According to John Lott, citizens need to take over some aspects of policing. He points out that police salaries and necessary resources were excessive, and they often did not work in a timely way to deter crime. But private citizens could invest in their own guns and receive immediate benefits from such ownership. What Lott called "nondiscretionary concealed-handgun laws" were the "most cost-effective means of reducing crime." In particular, Lott advocated that women, blacks, and the elderly invest in a gun and obtain a conceal-carry permit. The weakest were the most vulnerable and in need of the most acute private police power.[12]

Gun-rights advocates I've listened to take some pride in the image of their grandmas packing guns or their wives armed and ready to fire. The logic was invincible. Instead of a gun-free world, we should set our sights on a world in which each individual citizen is armed and ready, carrying on his or her body a concealed weapon to use when needed.

This endgame scenario of a gun utopia has created some tense conflicts in families, neighborhoods, and towns. For example, Benewah County, Idaho, close to where I live, tried to pass an ordinance requiring every household to have a working firearm. If all citizens were armed and required not only to carry an arm but also have a working firearm in their house, then a criminal would face clear and certain deterrents. What was defeated in Benewah County has been passed in a few towns in the United States like Kennesaw, Georgia and Virgin, Utah.[13] Claims about crime plummeting in Kennesaw have been posted on the Internet. But these ordinances have also been seen as political statements more than as enforceable laws. They were also specific reactions to an ordinance banning handguns in the city of Morton Grove, Illinois, in the early 1980s.[14] One city's ban led to another city's defiant act of requiring guns in the home. Mandatory-gun zones countered gun-free zones.

What fascinated Peter about the relationship between deterrents and crime was that it involved individual choice for both the citizen and the criminal. A criminal could choose to rob or not, and a citizen could choose to carry a concealed weapon or not. Peter insisted that he was an intellectual and that guns were not "political statements." They were deterrents, pure and simple, and, of course, as such they needed political protection. Peter described himself as "an idea person. Arguments are more important in political matters than force." He urged me again to read John Lott carefully. "No one has defeated his argument," he claimed, even though there is a cottage industry in the fields of sociology, criminology, political science, and legal studies that spends tidy sums of research monies on refuting Lott's claims. But here, I basically agreed with him. Ideas do have force, often more than the gun.

Working as an economist, Peter believed that strict limits on government protected individual freedom. He felt that many economists agreed with him and his insistence on rational choice. Free-enterprise capitalism worked well with his ideas. As long as an individual's actions did not "coerce other people," the individual "ought to be free." Peter was not a member of the National Rifle Association. He had not "fired a gun in six months." He was "more addicted to using a computer." Guns in the hands of individuals were a means to make the costs outweigh the benefits gained by robbery. It all came back to the economic scenario of someone breaking into your home.

Peter insisted that a burglar made a choice. He would make this choice based on costs and benefits. If the cost to him was a gunshot wound and the benefit a stolen TV, he would not break into the home. He would choose not to commit the crime. Put that way, it made perfect sense. Who would risk his life for a TV? You would have to be stupid, or on drugs, or desperate, or crazy. Put simply in terms of costs and benefits, it made sense. Guns were a deterrent. I could see those guys in prison shaking their heads.

Thinking back on that afternoon, I realized that Peter's ideas spun around in a logic of possibility, not probability, and certainly stayed clear of any responsibility for violence, any line drawn between fearing and the creation of fear. Rather, his intellectual position kept MAD alive in the minds of the average guy sitting in his living room somewhere in America, wondering about how to deter a criminal with as much firepower as he could get. Underneath the mass of statistics arguing that gun ownership and conceal-carry laws decrease crime lives an individual citizen who has lost faith in his society's ability to protect him; to provide human safety for its citizens. Gone were any conversations that would make crime a human dilemma that takes all of our best efforts to solve or reduce. Instead, the individual citizen practiced the strategy of MAD, arming to provide him- or herself with necessary police protection, a privatized police force of one.

That free-enterprise economists like Lott and Peter promoted this strategy was not surprising. We can no longer imagine the social, especially when the social appears with a face more unlike ours every day. Instead, as individual consumer-citizens, we act out a drama of fear, disengaged from social change that could promote the common well-being. In the economic language of this form of capitalism, protection is best defined as a deterrent that an individual citizen can buy—and buy quickly, with a minimum of regulation or requirements such as training, waiting periods, or background checks.

I live in a low-crime area in the rural West, as does Peter. Domestic violence, drunk driving, and the increasing use of methamphetamines are the real dangers facing my neighbors and me. Yet many of my neighbors are armed. Underemployment and lost dreams scar my landscape, a landscape of fear that depends not so much upon the immediate threat of danger as on the accumulation of everyday anxieties. The armed citizen lives under a Mad Max vision, unable to commit to the civil structures that would promote economic and social justice, but willing to retreat into the citadel of the citizen-consumer armed and ready to fire. The limits of our social beliefs are terrifying.

9

PURCHASING POWER

Gray December rain sprinkled the hundreds of pickups parked in straight rows in the Western Washington Fairgrounds parking lot. The folks inside the network of the long, low buildings normally used for poultry contests and quilt competitions were hunting for Christmas stocking stuffers. The ticket seller at the Puyallup Gun Show, the largest in western Washington, wore a drooping Santa hat. She took my five dollars and stamped my hand with purple ink. A red-and-white toy Santa was stretched spread-eagle, stuck to the glass window of her cubicle.

The gun show before Christmas drew a large crowd. Four thousand people would attend on a weekend. Between 250 and 300 exhibitors displayed guns, ammunition, knives, military surplus, clothing, jewelry, and books on between 750 and 1,000 tables. Puyallup had ten or eleven of these shows a year. There were at least fifty gun shows in the state of Washington annually, operated by a handful of organizers. About one three-day show every weekend.

This pattern would be repeated throughout the United States, with up to 5,000 shows held every year.[1] These gatherings have become political battlefields pitting gun show organizers, gun lobbyists, and NRA affiliates against unsympathetic members of Congress, government agencies, and state and municipal governments. Attempts to shut them down, curb their activities, or enforce regulations have resulted in charged confrontations in courtrooms and Congress. In October 1999, Los Angeles County tried to shut down a California gun show called the Great Western. After some negotiations, a final show was permitted for December in time for Christmas sales. Four years later, after legal battles with Los Angeles County and internal conflicts between the county and the Los Angeles County Fair Association, the show's organizers received $1.6 million from the county for lost revenues.[2] After some attempts to revive the Great Western under new organizers, the gun show folded for good. But that wasn't the end. State and federal lawsuits commenced, defending the gun show through arguments based on the First and Second Amendments to the Bill of Rights.

I've been told by a major gun-show organizer that the man who headed up the Great Western was a "free spirit" who didn't want to cooperate with local law enforcement.[3] With up to 5,000 tables, the Great Western show was difficult to monitor for illegal sales. It also made its organizers amazingly rich. The general manager of the Great Western has since taken his show to Texas. But the Great Western was a model for making money in the domestic market.

Gun shows generate income by renting an individual table to a single guy selling a few World War II arms or a block of tables to a commercial discount gun sale company. Three years ago, rent for an individual table ran anywhere from $40 to $60 per weekend, with additional fees for booths. Add that amount to the revenue collected from admission and you have a substantial figure even before a single gun is sold. One major gun-show organizer told me that the Great Western made its manager a multimillionaire.

Between 1985 and 1990, commercial shows expanded and started renting public fairgrounds. The only drawback to the entrepreneurial gun-show formula was the tough competition from other shows and the demographic that was served. As one organizer put it, "The number of gun shows continues to expand. The audience is not expanding." After all, how many new guns can you sell to the same people? How many guns can you exchange or trade?

Many gun shows are also forums for Second Amendment organizations, promoting an array of conservative political causes and candidates. David B. Kopel, a policy analyst at the conservative Cato Institute, contributing editor for *Gun Week*, and well-known gun-rights advocate, has objected to the "mean-spirited campaign of abuse" aimed at gun shows. He described the shows as "gathering points for people who are interested in Second Amendment issues" at which literature was distributed and members recruited for Second Amendment organizations.[4] A gun show is, indeed, a political fair.

I have walked the aisles at gun shows and heard announcements over the PA system telling the crowds to remember to vote for a conservative Republican up for election. Many conservatives come to pass out books, pamphlets, newsletters, and bumper stickers. These shows also can become effective means to register new NRA members and distribute information about that group's specific voting issues and political campaigns. They are truly linked to grassroots efforts to promote and protect gun rights and conservative politics.[5] Since the late 1980s, members of the NRA have received free admission to the Great Western show, and NRA volunteer groups have recruited at gun shows.

For many people I have talked with and interviewed, the act of buying a gun was in itself a political act. The purchase of a weapon was the very moment when they were able to exercise political freedom. I have one friend whose favorite line was "Whenever I get mad at the government, I go out and buy a gun." He was a resentful navy pilot who had served in the Vietnam War. To buy a gun in itself was the act of resistance against the government and its policies. Gun storeowners admit their good fortune when the government wants to ban a particular gun. Sales go way up, not only to beat the ban but also to defy the ban.

As with the purchase of other products deemed dangerous or illegal, the purchaser of a firearm was regulated. When you bought a pack of cigarettes or a case of beer, you might be asked to show an ID to prove you were over eighteen years old. The state established rules for buyers. In Washington at a gun show, you fill out a form, present an ID, undergo an Instant Background Check, and, if everything checks out, you are able to buy your gun. But the state's regulatory power over firearms was not a neutral issue for many men in the gun shows. The regulations were perceived by gun owners as an attempt by liberals and the Left to control their lives. Therefore, purchasing a gun meant you could defy the brand of politics that you despised.

The ease of buying guns has been a fact of life in the United States. Since World War II, gun purchases have risen steadily, peaking in 1993 at the time of the Brady Bill, with levels now the same as they were in the late 1980s. Four and a half million new gun sales take place in the United States each year.[6] We have a saturated market that requires intense advertising to generate additional sales.[7] In one way, the increase in gun sales says more about how consumers are manipulated than about how the gun buyer resists either the government or liberal politics. And further, the bumper-sticker language of political freedom attached to the gun has become an advertising gimmick to help foster sales. Advertising drives gun sales. And if guns can appear to promote specific political beliefs, so much the better for sales.

In this way, the gun has become a political fetish. It is what one cultural critic describes as a lie that helps us live with a disturbing truth.[8] At a time when access to political power is increasingly limited to a class of professional politicians, lobbyists, and moneyed elites, the act of buying a gun can mimic genuine political action. Gun shows are markets for these political pantomimes that simulate the exercise of political power with objects that seem to contain and convey personal power. It is not merely compensation for the loss of real access to politics. Gun purchasing is a redirection of energy to perpetuate a political system that disempowers the buyer.

I call these purchases the gun closet of our political and social failures. Ideology aside, what are most guns used for in the United States? Hunting has been steadily diminishing, and the huge numbers of guns produced in the U.S. have little, if any, relationship with the hunting sports. Target practicing has become increasingly difficult as ranges have become difficult to find. Self-defense has always been a strong selling point. And killing, of course, has kept pace with drug trafficking, bank robberies, and physical assaults. The incidence of accidents with firearms is high in the United States, especially among young people and children. In fact, many handguns in United States are not used to kill a burglar or an estranged spouse, but are used to commit suicide. White men over fifty-five are the most vulnerable group. Women try to kill themselves three times more often than do men, but men succeed four times more often than women because men—especially white men—own guns. In his recent book, *Private Guns, Public Health,* David Hemenway writes that almost "fifty people a day kill themselves with guns in the United States. These numbers increased 75 percent between 1965 and 1985 and have stayed reasonably constant since then."[9] Hemenway also writes that half a million Americans have been murdered with guns since 1960,[10] but since 1965 the same number have committed suicide with guns, more than ten times the number killed by gun accidents.[11] In some ways, the most common lethal use of a gun in the United States is a white man killing himself.

In our national gun closet, guns have become constitutionally protected products; it's our citizens who have been left out in the cold. Arms manufacturers drum on the Constitution to avoid their social responsibility. The gun-rights movement supports arms manufacturers in their lax monitoring of their dealers, and this allows the dumping of as many guns as possible into the domestic and global markets. The arms industry and the NRA have plenty of attorneys and lobbyists to make sure your constitutionally protected product and their manufacturers can operate, or be operated, with immunity. Robert Ricker, the whistleblower of the arms manufacturers, has testified that reasonable measures to have manufacturers sell to "certified dealers" have been rejected by key players who travel between Washington, D.C. lobbying work and corporate boardrooms.[12]

In 1999, Ricker was the executive director of the American Shooting Sports Council (ASSC), which merged with the National Shooting Sports Foundation (NSSF).[13] During the merger, his desire to reform the industry met with opposition. He resigned and has since testified about how the arms manufacturers do business.

Several cities have tried to sue arms manufacturers in attempts to get them to sell only to "certified dealers."[14] In these suits, crime guns have been traced to specific dealers in their communities.[15] In fact, the idea of selling to "certified dealers" was brought up by people like Ricker who were inside the arms manufacturing world, arguing for more accountability. Cities have also asked for other measures, like making serial numbers difficult to remove. In these lawsuits, the question always arose: why did arms manufacturers keep selling to dealers whose guns kept ending up in the hands of criminals? Insiders have testified that the arms manufacturers knew about the problem. Only under pressure have manufacturers started to ask their dealers to watch for "straw purchases," purchases made by legal buyers that were handed over to illegal buyers. Many states have passed laws against such purchases. These lawsuits revealed that the legal gun market supports an illicit gun market. When the legal market is saturated to such an extent—as it is in the United States—guns find their way into the hands of people unable to purchase them legally—especially young men.

These debates were buried in the pages of lawsuits. The NRA had a loud voice; attempts to carry out a public debate over these social problems have been drowned out by Second Amendment alarmists and the army of volunteers who rise up to protect gun rights. Patriotism stands behind the gun buyer. Gun rights silence the open discussion of how guns function in our

communities and what reasonable means a community can take
to ensure that its citizens are not under unnecessary threat. But
if politics can be equated with a gun purchase, that discussion
is rendered irrelevant.

The small town at the edge of the Cascades Mountains in
Washington State runs about ten gun shows a year at its fairgrounds. The air was damp and cold on this November day. It
took a few minutes for my husband and me to find the entrance
through the maze of buildings. Once inside, I looked out over
the large pavilion room and across the exhibits to a sea of men's
heads, in clusters and alone, staring at ammunition, guns, leather
holsters, and videos on safety and survival.

I was only in the show about five minutes before I ran into
the table with the "most unique firearm on earth," the .50 caliber rifle in different variations of single-shot and five-shot.
Depending upon accessories like bench rest, spotting scope,
bipod, tripod, and case, I could walk home with this new hit,
the "ultimate sniper rifle," for anywhere between $3,000 and
$7,500. The .50 caliber was the baddest gun in town, pushing
aside the old MAC-10s and military-style rifles found sprinkled
throughout the show.

I'm not sure who buys the "ultimate sniper rifle" at these
shows. I didn't see one purchased. I kept wondering if there
were undercover cops in the pavilion keeping track. The state of
California recently went through a battle over whether this
firearm should be manufactured, distributed, imported, or owned
within its borders. Seen as a potential terrorist weapon, the gun
was described in hearings as a potent threat. Worries about its
use against civilian airports and nuclear facilities fueled argu-

ments against the rifle's proponents, who stood fast behind the Second Amendment.[16]

The gun was used in the Gulf War by the military, has amazing accuracy at long distances, and can pierce multiple layers of metal. Of course, that's what makes it so enjoyable and challenging to shoot, claim its owners. The Fifty Caliber Shooters Association boasts a high education level for their members and organizes competitive shoots between ten and fifteen times a year on its 1,000-yard range, that's almost ten football fields.

The .50 caliber rifle even had an institute to plead its Second Amendment case, the Fifty Caliber Shooters Policy Institute. The institute's website stated that their "sport has been demonized by several anti-gun legislators who are using the fifty caliber rifle as a means to take all firearms away from the American public."[17] They insisted that ordinary criminals never used the gun. It was too big and too expensive. Law-abiding citizens with Second Amendment rights should have the right to buy and shoot the rifle. But opponents of the gun continued to stress the lack of regulation for such a powerful weapon that has been used effectively by military and international terrorist organizations. Classified as a "long rifle," the .50 caliber escaped regulation imposed on sawed-off shotguns and machine guns.

There were a number of different .50 caliber rifles to be found at the gun show. People hung around and looked at the black gun propped up on a bipod. The advertising went straight to the point. It was the "ultimate weapon," like the ultimate lipstick or the ultimate sports car. Some even wanted to pick it up and hold it. After all, its destructive power was an instant thrill.

Guns touch and tempt. They are the closest some people will get to the immediate physical sensation of raw power. Even if you were only shooting a target or a bowling pin or, like some people I know, a stick of dynamite, shooting can be exciting.

Guns bring you close to the adrenaline rush of violence and acts of destruction. If you don't have extensive training, they easily short-circuit your chance to think. How immediate. How fast. Just a squeeze, and the gun goes off.

And unlike the guns of hunters, sport shooters, and even pretend cowboys, the new military-style guns are a cultural doorway into special-ops fantasies, with soldiers of fortune adrift on the planet, shooting bad guys in Third World landscapes as they do in so many computer games. Many critics, like James William Gibson and Susan Jeffords, have written about the paramilitary culture of hypermasculinity that arose in the 1980s and has stayed with us to the present.[18] But this new warrior guy presents some unique problems to the Second Amendment advocates who use the Constitution to protect their products.

Interviewing younger men and women who grew up in the 1980s, I have remarked on the allure of the pop-culture warrior. One man in his thirties told me about how his friends and he would pass around *Soldier of Fortune* magazine in junior high and high school to check out the latest weapons.[19] Military-style guns, that's what they were into. He and his friends never subscribed to the magazine; they wanted to be invisible. He wasn't an alienated youth without friends. He and his friends were the kids in school who were into guns. He lived in the rural West, and guns were part of the culture. But he didn't think his parents knew how much he was into guns. During school, his group would decide to go out shooting. They'd go home and gather their weapons and head up the canyon to target practice. All the guns were unloaded. The rifles were on the back seat, the pistols under the seat. The kids were under twenty-one, and it was illegal to own a handgun in their state. But they all did. It was illegal to buy ammunition for a handgun, but they all did. It was like booze. Drinking was illegal too. But they all did.

They never did anything illegal with the guns. Though they did fantasize once about taking over the high school. But that was just a fantasy.

The movie *Red Dawn* really made an impression. It featured Russians taking over a high school in a small Colorado town and a group of students headed by Patrick Swayze becoming freedom fighters, guerrilla warriors, hiding in the mountains. Released in 1984, the movie was a big hit with his guy friends. They were all against registration of guns. If a foreign invasion happened, the enemy could come to your home and seize your weapons. You had to hide your guns from the "bad people" who would take over the government. You weren't hiding your guns from the government. But it was always best to "stay below radar."

New movies brought new guns. *The Terminator. The Dogs of War.* They were hits. The kids' "taste would change, depending upon what movie was the rage." They'd drive over to the closest gun show, ninety rural minutes away by car, to check out "military-style rifles and handguns." The gun shows he went to in the 1980s were filled mainly with military surplus. They were not like a "gun store," as they are today. He remembered the smell of Hoppe's gun solvent and musty fatigues. Mildew. They were into the "mystique of the soldier of fortune." One in the group did join the Army and became a sniper. There was a lot of military recruiting out of high school, which is common in the rural West.

By the end of high school, he and his friends had quite a collection of guns. Some they had purchased by trading up at gun shows. They weren't very good at trading. They knew they were being taken, but they didn't really care. They were "high school kids being taken to the cleaners, but we wanted a new toy. No ifs or ands about it. We knew we were taking a hit."

The collection was international, no made-in-the-U.S.A. worries at all. A Valmet Model 76 Assault 7.62, the Finnish military rifle perfected from the Russian workhorse AK-47. A Steyr AUG, the Austrian assault rifle, developed for the Austrian army. Considered a commercial success, this rifle has been used by the armed forces in Australia, Austria, New Zealand, Oman, Malaysia, Saudi Arabia, and Ireland. A SPAS-12, the shotgun developed by an Italian company for military and police close combat. An Uzi, the Israeli submachine gun adapted to various pistol and semiautomatic specifications, modeled after a Czech submachine gun. An AK-47, the famous assault rifle with the banana-shaped magazine, originally from Russia but now produced by dozens of countries. Inexpensive to manufacture, it has been one of the most common guns to be used in conflicts around the globe since the end of World War II. An SKS, the semiautomatic rifle adopted by the Soviet Union in 1946 and the precurser to the AK-47. And last but not least, a MAC-10, the gun that seems to defy categories in terms of its lethality and the ease with which it can be changed from semi to fully automatic, but which in terms of legal catagories is a handgun.

The guns were too expensive for a high school kid. He had to be "more practical." He "lived vicariously" through his friends, and they would share the guns. He admitted that they were "gun snobs." They used to laugh at "knock-off" guns like the TEC-9. What "a piece of shit." They had between them several handguns, a Browning Hi-Power, a Desert Eagle, and a Beretta. After a gun show, they couldn't wait to drive all the way home. They would "stop at a gravel pit on the way back and target practice with the new toys." They were "trying to be responsible. They would never add to the trash after shooting. They cleaned up."

Did it end, I asked, this interest in guns?

"Oh, yes. When I moved to the big city, I wasn't around my peer group."

It did take some time to change. At first he lived in a racially mixed neighborhood. A higher-crime area. For three months he carried a pistol with him. He had a conceal-carry permit. But nothing happened. "Honestly, I don't think people need guns for home protection. It's better to have few guns in the inner city. I could not personally choose a firearm for personal protection at this time in my life. In my neighborhood, if someone starting going around shooting people, I might get a gun. But I'm a big guy. I don't have security issues." He told me "anyone with half a brain can avoid violence."

He admitted that he might "hesitate" to use a gun for personal protection. That would be bad. No, he knew he would use his "paintball gun" against an intruder. He could get off a bunch of shots fast. Not like most of the legal guns that are single-shot or semiautomatic. A flurry of paintball shots would bring down anybody. He wouldn't hesitate. If you have a gun, you must be willing to use it. No hesitation.

He still liked to play paintball games. He'd drive out to the mountains once in a while and spend the afternoon trying to track and ping the opponents. Sometimes there were kids as young as fourteen in the game. It was a lot of fun.

No, you didn't need a gun for home protection.

I asked him about the Second Amendment.

When he was a teenager, the only issue was registration. His gun buddies were Democrats and Republicans. His one Indian friend was a hardcore Republican. Really into Reagan. Their politics boiled down to registration.

Today, he thought it was "up to the lawyers to decide that legalese." He didn't think the Second Amendment justified "assault weapons to the populace." It was for the "lawyers and judges to decide."

He thought gun rights were of "moderate importance." He did not think of it daily, but he "would miss it if it was gone." He was much more concerned about "fair and equal taxes." He wanted to "tax the rich." He was more concerned about civil rights and freedom of speech. He felt he would use his gun to defend the Constitution, but he would rank civil rights "much higher than the right to own a gun. Civil equality."

Tom, who had organized gun shows for decades, was worried that the younger guys weren't thinking straight. They weren't as committed to politics. They were into "entertainment." He and other gun-show organizers had told me that they had to work on political education. The gun show, he said, was an important forum for "political expression." The threats to gun owners were real. The graying of the gun-rights movement was worrisome. The moral glow of ownership was missing if you couldn't tie it to national identity and the fight for freedom.

There was among gun rights advocates a continual worry about the power of the movies. And they had reason to be worried. One man I interviewed had grown up in the gun culture of the 1990s, gone to gun shows every weekend, and eventually managed a gun store. He would watch the latest movie releases to guide his gun orders. He would also use "politics to sell guns," even though he considered himself nonpolitical. At one point, he owned "over five hundred" firearms. And now he wanted out of what he considered a "culture of death and fear," having watched his "addiction" to guns escalate.[20] The cultural hysteria of the 1960s was a long way away from the twenty-first century, and gun rights needed a stream of internal and external enemies to keep the good fight going. Young men had to see how owning guns was an exercise in political freedom. Patriotism needed to be the grease in the rifle's barrel. A civilian locked and loaded. But too many young guys just wanted to play.

The old 1970s moral and political rationales for gun ownership that had been found in clever interpretations of the Second Amendment had begun to wear thin and belonged more to a world of aging white men. Buffalo Bill had found his match in Rambo. The gun as a political fetish had returned through popular culture to a fantasy of sheer power, firing in the world of international villains with little moral persuasion other than brute force.

The World War II veteran, the Cold War anti-Communist, the disgruntled Vietnam War hawk all had to compete with PlayStation global warriors, those first-person shooters who liked to pull the trigger. Tom Diaz has written that about half the guns "available to civilians between 1899 and 1993 (forty-six percent) were produced between 1974 and 1993."[21] The post-1974 market that brought with it the political mantra of gun rights initiated a two-decades-long buying spree. That spree left some young men without the moral passions of the previous generation, who had seen the world through the conservative political filter of crime, threat, and defiance. To the next generation, guns were mainly about fun, cool, and power.

PART FOUR

10

GUN-GRABBING WIVES

He was much larger than I am, and he had a beefy football-player build and short dark hair—the bouncer type. He was going to get physical if I objected. He was ready to push as we walked quickly past the long row of tables covered with guns and ammo, past the woman collecting money for admission. Talk to him, I said to myself. Talk to him. I kept telling him I didn't work for the newspapers as he herded me to the exit.

"No pictures," he kept repeating.

"No pictures," he insisted one last time as he opened the heavy door and gently pushed me out. Then he closed the door and left me standing outside with my camera dangling from my hand.

A hand-lettered sign appeared outside the entrance: NO CAMERAS ALLOWED.

Thirty minutes earlier I had walked into the public fairgrounds to attend a local gun show in Moscow, Idaho. It was the mid 1990s, and I was taking photographs of abandoned lumber mills and deserted mines in the Pacific Northwest. I was shooting what I thought were the industrial ruins of the rural West. I had also taken pictures of men in gun stores eyeing a new rifle and men hunting during deer and elk season, the ordinary lives of rural Westerners. I wanted to add pictures of men and women at gun shows.

At that point, I wasn't writing about gun culture. I was only taking pictures of daily life in small rural Western towns.

My husband eventually found me outside. We talked about what had happened and decided to find out if it was legal to prevent me from taking photographs at a gun show held at a public fairground. We phoned around and received conflicting answers from city and county attorneys.

The phone system in the small town was working well that day. By the time we came back to the gun show to talk with the organizer, an unofficial compromise had been reached with the relevant public officials. I could come back the next morning with my camera and photograph before the public was admitted. I could photograph the exhibitors and their exhibits if I asked permission first and they agreed.

I was disappointed, of course. What I wanted to shoot was the feel of the gun show. How people held guns, bargained with sellers, traded, and shopped for guns. I wanted to inch closer to why guns were so important to rural Westerners. I wasn't certain what I would find.

I agreed to the conditions. Some pictures are better than none.

Before I left, I asked the organizer why they enforced rules against cameras. What was the problem? Was it a distrust of government? Did they think I worked for the ATF, the IRS, or the FBI? Was it anger against gun-control groups? Did they think I worked for Sarah Brady's handgun organization, or for Cease Fire, a Seattle-based gun violence prevention group? Maybe it was about hunting and animal rights? Or worse, I could be a PETA worker.

There was a long list of possible reasons for the no-camera policy.

The organizer looked at me hard when I asked the question. Why no cameras? He responded with one word: "Alimony."

"What?" I asked. Had I heard right?

"Alimony?"

"Yes, alimony." He then explained that the men inside the gun show didn't want their pictures showing up in newspapers where their ex-wives might see them.

I asked him more questions, but he wasn't in a talking mood. It was about alimony, period. I'd have to leave it at that.

Maybe the organizer thought some ex-wife had hired me to track down her husband and prove that he was handing over for a new hunting rifle what should be her cash. Maybe the organizer actually thought that ex-wives scanned the local papers looking for photos of their former husbands to see if they could catch them spending what was legally theirs.

At later gun shows, I started to pay more attention. Were ex-wives and their demands a threat to some guys at the gun shows? I frequently saw books for sale at the shows such as *The Predatory Female* by Rev. Lawrence Shannon, whose field guide to dating includes a set of tactics to undermine the supposed Gestapo power of women who rule the divorce and child-custody judicial system. In a radio interview, Shannon said that "victims of the predatory female are strewn all over the nation, writing alimony checks, recovering from gunshot wounds, treating cat scratches, trying to see their children, paying attorney's fees, picking through the detritus of their lives, and struggling to recover from ruined years."[1] *The Predatory Female* is a collection of warnings about women who prey on the feelings and bank accounts of unsuspecting men. Female predators have their eyes on one thing alone—money. They marry and divorce to get alimony. They use emotions of love, trust, and care to undermine the sacred contract of marriage. They are the new scourges of secular life, hunting down unsuspecting men to get bucks and tear out their hearts.

Wives were threats. Girlfriends were threats. Women who talked too much were threats. And women who held public office and wouldn't shut up were the scourge of the land. I have also picked up bumper stickers at gun shows that said: I JUST GOT A GUN FOR MY WIFE. IT'S THE BEST TRADE I EVER MADE. Or handouts detailing the "Top 10 Reasons Handguns Are Better than Women," ending with the number-one reason, "You can buy a silencer for a handgun." I had also seen some pretty vicious materials on Hillary Clinton and Janet Reno at local shows in the '90s. A new fear floated above some of the gun exhibits: judges, lawyers, and voters were giving women too much power, and the women were using that power to take guns away from their husbands, their boyfriends, and their constituents. A gun-grabber lurked in the heart of the liberated woman.

Maybe the no-camera rule was about alimony. In this latest male fantasy about the war between the sexes, I could have been hired by a female predator to shoot pictures at a gun show for a ruthless ex- or estranged wife. I was just part of a new generation of bottom-feeders out to get men, one of the vast army of women intent on misandry, a new word invented to capture this hatred of men by women.

At the law seminar in Reno during the 2002 National Rifle Association annual convention, I learned about other ways women can grab guns. The atmosphere in the hotel conference room exuded professionalism, with somber and rational panels on topics such as Constitutional and criminal law, nonprofit and tax-exempt information, product liability, and ethics. Sitting in the darkened room, listening to the intricacies of product liability defense, I thought about the contrast in tone between the pumped-up speeches in the other rooms at the hotel and the subdued discussions of the lawyers, policy analysts, and historians working for the NRA. In the midst of these carefully paced presentations, I first heard about the legal problems gun owners dealt with when faced with domestic-violence orders.

Under the terms of certain restraining orders, guns are prohibited. Domestic violence and divorce set in motion a range of both state and federal statutes and laws aimed at disarming violent or potentially violent intimate partners. Since the 1996 Lautenberg Amendment that followed passage of the Violence Against Women Act in 1994, it is a federal crime to possess a firearm while subject to a restraining order from an intimate partner or after a misdemeanor conviction of the crime of domestic violence.[2]

No one at the law seminar lingered on why there was domestic violence in the United States, or how this violence affected men, women, and children, or what steps could be taken to reduce or prevent such violence. And for many of the attorneys present, it was strictly a legal issue about due process, federal statutes, and legal precedents.³ What happened in the living room or bedroom, likely sites of what crime analysts called simple assault, was off the political and rhetorical radar screens. At the law seminar I also heard no discussions on how to protect women from men in their own homes. No, the issue was only about how many individuals convicted of misdemeanors or strapped with restraining orders would lose the right to own firearms. The big issue was how to get them back. It was all about the guns.

I found out that the police were particularly vulnerable. There was mention of how the Minneapolis Police Department was practically disarmed because so many police had present or past restraining orders against them. There was a sense of relief that the courts and Congress might rule in favor of the cops and military personnel, exempting them from the gun regulation. No one talked about domestic violence, because violence in the home didn't have the emotional punch of a violent predator breaking into your home. Then the homeowner was a hero defending his property, not a villain beating up on his spouse. The vigilante gun owner could hang a sign in his window, announcing IS THERE LIFE AFTER DEATH? TRESPASS HERE AND FIND OUT. Or, WARNING!! TRESPASSERS WILL BE SHOT. SURVIVORS WILL BE SHOT AGAIN. But what kind of sign could the battered wife hang up?

In 2005, Ted Nugent, in his keynote address to the NRA annual meeting in Houston, could rant about plugging all the bad guys: "I want 'em dead." But what if the cop or the soldier or the store-owner was the bad guy? Cops were a touchy subject in gun-rights circles. Some police organizations wanted exceptions made for officers under restraining orders, which would make it more difficult for them to lose their firearms. There were complicated legal questions about restraining orders and previous misdemeanor convictions of domestic violence. Other cops wanted "law enforcement persons" held to a "higher standard, not a different standard." In 1997, Ronald E. Hampton, the executive director of the National Black Police Association, testified before the House Subcommittee on Crime. He spoke against exempting police officers. "At a time when the relationship between the community and the police is constantly deteriorating, we believe this effort by police unions and other associations is misguided and will result in the continued widening gulf between the community and the police." He went on to say in 1995, "forty percent of police questioned acknowledged using physical force with a partner in the past year."[4] According to other testimony, police and military personnel were implicated in the crime of domestic violence at higher rates than were the general population. The Domestic Violence Offender Gun Ban provides no exemptions for these two groups.

One gun lobbyist I interviewed lowered his voice when he told me—off the record—that he had no sympathy for the cop who loses his gun to a restraining order. He had scolded one cop who called him up, telling him he wanted nothing to do with the cop's restraining-order complaint. But he wanted me to know that he felt women overreacted with restraining orders: women were abusing their new power in the courts, leaving men defenseless without their guns. Discussions of crime seemed always to come back to crimes by strangers who used or might use violent force. Once again, the armed assailant seemed to be the major threat—indeed, the only threat. But there was that one nagging exception, the man who turned on his partner with rage.

In 1998, the National Institute for Justice reported that each year 1.5 million women were raped or physically assaulted

by intimate partners. Many of these attacks occurred in the pri-
vacy of the home. Men were more likely to be attacked by
strangers. In contrast, women were seven to fourteen times
"more likely to report that an intimate partner beat them up,
choked or tried to drown them, threatened them with a gun, or
actually used a gun on them."[5]

As a woman at gun shows, I am usually pitched specific
guns to ward off the predator breaking into my house or stalking
me. At a gun show in the state of Washington, I spent time talking with an arms manufacturer who specialized in variations of
the AR-15, originally made by Colt. A semiautomatic rifle that
has parts interchangeable with the M16, this rifle can accom-
modate a number of different calibers and setups. It has been
modified so that it cannot be interchangeable in its lower receiver group with M16 parts, making it difficult to give it full
automatic capability.

The marketing specialist at the booth told me that the AR-15
could be adapted for home defense. I could put in a short barrel, less than 16" long—what cops used in closed spaces to
shoot the bad guys. The man at the booth warned me that he
couldn't put the short barrel in the gun receiver because he
would be breaking the law. No barrel under 16" can go into
the gun frame. Instead, he held it about a half-inch from the
gun frame and demonstrated how it would work. It was an
impressive-looking weapon. Stocky and mean, a dull black.

I wanted to ask him if he was serious. Did he really think I
would buy a military weapon to defend my home? I always
thought if you really had cause to worry about an intruder in
your bedroom, and there was no way you could run, you'd yank
the shotgun out from the closet and blast away. You wouldn't
even have to aim. You wouldn't even have to use buckshot. The
noise from rock salt would scare most people to death. But he

looked calm and intent, and I wasn't about to get into a quarrel with him about his goods.

Only once do I remember a salesman trying to sell me a gun to shoot my husband or boyfriend if he turned abusive. His personal philosophy on life was that everyone should be armed and packing. If everyone in the world were armed, there would be no domestic violence; in fact, there would be no violence at all. The bad husbands would finally get what they deserved. And all the bad people in the world would be stopped—killed or executed on the spot. He insisted that even everyone in a bar, the traditional hot spot for assault, should be packing heat. Forget about alcohol. The gun itself would stop the violence. So what if the guy packing was drunk out of his skull? The gun had this amazing magic to prevent violence. It was a talisman of peace. I had reached the logical end of the gun-rights argument. Stop crime: Arm everyone.

Yet something was desperately wrong with this picture, even though I knew that some women, fearing for their lives every day, have decided to arm themselves against their ex-loved ones. Overall, domestic violence took the glamour out of the crime scene that pro-gun activists loved to describe. Husbands and wives shooting it out in the living room didn't have the same appeal as the brave homeowner gunning down a crazed burglar. And what about all those ad campaigns to get me to buy guns? The magazine and book tales of masked young predators generated gun sales. How do you advertise buying guns when the criminal was an ex-husband, a boyfriend, or a guy you dated a couple of weeks ago?

At the law seminar, I sat thinking about how much the right to own a gun owed to the typical crime-scene scenario. Those millions of hours that Americans spent watching cop shows and vigilante heroes helped pump up the psychic investment in guns. Still, I was having a hard time understanding how teams of lawyers for the National Rifle Association and other gun groups were ready to defend men under restraining orders. Maybe I just wasn't listening right.

At one point a question came up about Attorney General John Ashcroft and his push in the Department of Justice to accept the Second Amendment as an individual right. We were told that the Emerson case would determine whether Ashcroft's position would hold. Over the next couple of years, everywhere I turned in the gun-rights world the Emerson case was heralded as a great Second Amendment victory. Second Amendment activists would hand me copies of the complete legal ruling in paperback form. I have read on dozens of Second Amendment websites praise for the wisdom of the federal judges who wrote a masterly defense of individual rights. It was the greatest news to hit the gun lobby in years.

It came down to this: in 1998, the wife of Timothy Joe Emerson filed for divorce and applied for a restraining order against her husband. At a hearing, Sacha Emerson alleged that her husband made a threat over the telephone. He threatened to kill her "friend." The restraining order was granted. Later, her husband was indicted for "possession of a firearm while being under a restraining order." But, in a Texas federal district court, this indictment was dismissed by Judge Sam R. Cummings. In a memorandum brimming with colonial history, the Second Amendment reared its righteous head. Judge Cummings argued that the federal actions to protect women against intimate-partner violence didn't hold up against the struggles of our revolutionary fathers to found a nation with arms. The estranged and threatening husband had a sacred and individual right to his guns. No "boilerplate state court divorce order can collaterally and automatically extinguish a law-abiding citizen's Second Amendment rights."[6]

The government appealed to the federal Fifth Circuit Court, which upheld the indictment against the husband. The husband's attorneys argued that there were insufficient judicial findings that he was a "credible threat"; the Fifth Circuit Court disagreed. Two of the three judges accepted the argument that while the Second Amendment gave an individual a right to own a gun, it did not give an individual under a restraining order the right to own a gun.[7]

Gun activists sometimes lament the fact that it was hard to find a "righteous gun case" that they can take all the way up to the Supreme Court and prove once and for all that the Constitution protects the right of the individual to keep and bear arms. A gun used to threaten and intimidate a spouse was hardly a gun worth Constitutional protection. A gun brandished to scare a burglar was one thing; a gun brandished to scare a wife was another.

Was Sacha Emerson just another gun-grabbing wife? In reading the opinion of the Fifth Circuit Court, I wondered, because most of the opinion was not about the restraining order at all. That question was settled in a concise statement by the judges. Why this case was the great hope of the gun-rights world rested on the fact that two of the three federal judges had used the opinion to expound for more than fifty pages about how the Second Amendment protected individual rights. It was a coup d'état. There were also fourteen amicus curiae, or "friends of the court," submitting briefs to argue for Timothy Joe Emerson, including one from the National Rifle Association. And the arguments of the NRA's lawyers, or what is called their "2A" attorneys, and the two federal judges overlapped. I wasn't surprised. At meetings of the NRA, including their law seminar, I had repeatedly heard these legal opinions, especially arguments focused on what our founding fathers said or didn't say about the right to bear arms.[8] I guess the two federal judges were hoping that the Supreme Court would jump on their position and finally give the gun-rights activists what they had been claiming in their brand of conservative politics for thirty years. The final, sweet vindication by the highest court in the land seemed within reach.[9] The prize was finally in sight. Who cared if some frightened wife in Texas was worried enough to get a restraining order? She was probably overreacting. She didn't need protection; his gun did.

I wonder how Sacha Emerson reacted to this court drama. Her application for a restraining order set off a series of events that cranked up the gun-rights groups for years. They submitted briefs for her husband's position and even set up legal defense funds for his support. He was the man of the hour. He was the case that could go all the way.

Yet John Ashcroft never did win vindication through the Emerson case. The United States Supreme Court refused to hear any further appeals, a decision that depressed gun-rights activists for weeks. The legal teams of the National Rifle Association and other gun-rights groups would have to wait longer for their triumph in the Supreme Court.

11

ARMING GOD'S NATION

I once asked a gun-rights organizer if he spent much time trying to include fundamentalist Christians in his efforts to win
over adherents to his conservative political causes.[1] He basically
told me that he didn't think "gun rights did well in the Christian
Right if you look at various mailing lists." But that "didn't matter." He "had the Christian Right anyway." What became clearer
the more we talked was that the gun-rights movement to him
was only one of several ways to create and sustain social and political change in the United States. Guns, God, anti-abortion
and anti-gay organizations, tax reform, and a laissez-faire belief
in capitalism were catalysts that energized a shared conservative
vision for America. They were the revolutionary means to defeat
what was labeled as liberalism.

The gun-rights organizer's ideas became clearer to me when

I interviewed and talked with Christians who equated gun ownership with political freedom. The journalist David A. Neiwert
and others have followed how these ideological strands merge
into what is called the "Patriot Movement," mixing racist beliefs, Christian identity, and an armed, militant, and paranoid
politics that most Americans would find "repellent."[2] These
"crackpot" right-wing groups that Neiwert tracked in the Pacific
Northwest have often been the bane of conservative causes in
the United States. The Young Americans for Freedom in the
1960s and '70s consistently tried to distinguish their organization from the John Birch Society and several violent and racist
organizations like the Ku Klux Klan.[3]

Today, some groups like the Montana Human Rights Watch
would insist that the crackpots have found a voice in mainstream politics, and that extremists now advise mainstream politicians, particularly in relationship to gun rights. One example
was the 2003 Liberty Summit in Missoula, Montana, that brought
together Republican Party members, the gun lobby, and the Patriot Movement with such speakers as John Trochmann, Gary
Marbut, and Frank McGee.[4]

But as I talked with religious gun owners, I often found ordinary Americans trying to make sense of what they believed
was a decadent and dying society.[5] To them, America needed
change, and evangelical religion was a potent and necessary
force for a renewal of core American values. To the resurgent religious Right, the ecumenical impulse of the 1960s—which
opened American-style Christianity to other faiths and religious
expressions—had betrayed the true faith of the American nation.[6] Martin Luther King, Jr., traveling to India in search of
Gandhi, personified a dangerous religious attitude that looked
beyond American shores for faith that should be anchored in a
national Christian mission. Buddhism, New Age, and paganism

only hastened America's transformation into a spiritual waste-
land, where foreign gods tempted the true believer.

Further, some conservative Christians turned to national
politics and gun rights to promote what they believed was the
religious foundation of the nation. The Second Amendment
was a call to arms to sustain the fundamental vision of the
United States as God's nation. The gun protected the freedoms
of the citizen in a sacred society. Guns became the anointed
means to guarantee and uphold the core beliefs of this Christian country. Not merely a clever campaign tactic for conservative Republican organizers out to beat their opponents in state
and federal elections, gun rights were the righteous proof of
God's revelations to man throughout history.

One person that I interviewed, who did not belong to any
militia organization or to the Patriot Movement, expressed this
fusion with passion. He had merely spent much time thinking
about why his right to own guns was ordained by God. A teacher
in a private school, Gregory insisted that "Gun ownership is not
a belief. It is a God-given right." There was a "difference in liking arms and the right to own. Liking is a hobby, a personal
taste." What was more important was to understand that gun
rights came directly from God. "The right is to protect the self,
not given by government, not given by the Constitution, a God-
given right, my concept of God. If I don't believe in God, then I
don't believe in rights given by God, then they are only given by
a benevolent dictator." He believed in "God and Christ and the
God of the Bible."

Gregory's vision was utterly nationalistic. In its purest form,
the United States was the country that affirmed his belief that
rights "are not given by man." And the United States as the land
of the free had a special relationship to the Biblical Ten Commandments: The "First Commandment is the first command-

ment of liberty." God commanded man to worship and obey no other gods, and through this obedience came liberty and gun rights. "God," Gregory argued, "is either the author of liberty or the author of slavery." All other religions "practice a certain amount of servitude," bowing to the "gods of the slave masters." Only in Christianity can you "see the truth and the truth shall make you free."

My afternoon with Gregory convinced me of the enduring power of nationalism to create both identity and meaning, affirmed by a mandate given by God. Modern national states have often based their origin stories or births on premodern tribal roots that privilege a specific ethnic group, such as the founding fathers.[7] Citizens are granted rights by descent from this group. There is often tension between civil rights and these ethnic identities that guarantee citizens the protection of law through secular and written constitutions. Citizens have been granted rights through social contracts, compacts, and covenants. Belonging to a nation does not come about through the most visceral feelings—those of blood identity—but through human constructions written on paper that arrange governments to represent the people in ways that often seek to control the dark sides of human nature: greed, violence, abuse.

But some nations push the religious origins of their society with a vengeance, privileging a specific creed as the spiritual soul of the nation. In the United States, a providential history of our founding as a nation was often located within the colonial past of the English Puritans with their interest in covenants, but these religious roots were often exclusionary and punitive to those who did not share that faith. Some historians argue that when John Winthrop preached his Puritan sermon to the small group of believers on board the *Arabella* in 1630, the religious mission of the United States was born.

Other historians find that the Massachusetts Bay Colony became a "city upon a hill" for fellow Englishmen back home to imitate. They were super-patriots not of a new nation but of the old. The Puritans were suspicious of evangelicals and *deeply* suspicious of people who claimed to have direct access to the words of God. After all, they could be lying, deluded, or even in the clutches of Satan. And they could cause trouble for the church leaders.

With evangelicals like the Baptists and Methodists came religious enthusiasm, and evangelistic religions found fertile ground in the frontier communities of New England and the mid-Atlantic colonies. The Great Awakening of the eighteenth century, the burned-over districts of the nineteenth century, the itinerant preachers in small towns, and the small groups of prophets whose revelations led to such religions as Christian Science, Seventh-Day Adventists, and Mormons were hardly anomalies in American history. Many believed in millennialism and mapped out a geographical area of the United States in which to live and practice their particular brand of utopian beliefs.[8]

As a settler society, the United States has engaged in massive rhetorical justifications for its right to possess its lands in the Western Hemisphere. Religion helped the cause, raising the church steeple, the flag, and the fort as it moved progressively westward. There is a strain of thought in the United States that positions this nation as the purest expression of God in history. God gave the country's citizens inalienable rights, and with the light of God, the United States had not only accepted these inalienable rights but also wrote a Bill of Rights that was likened to the Ten Commandments. Each man had the responsibility to guarantee that these rights were upheld and enforced.

Since the renewed interest in the Second Amendment during the 1970s, a conservative religious language has arisen to justify gun ownership. The Second Amendment not only guaranteed the right to gun ownership; more important, it provided the "teeth" that individual citizens could use to enforce these rights. Each citizen should accept this responsibility of enforcement. Neither the police nor the military were entirely trustworthy or reliable. The light shone directly from God to the people. The sanctified gun owner directly enforced the Bill of Rights. He was an armed citizen granted direct access to political truth, and he could bypass the messy and conflicting interpretations made by lawyers, politicians, and the courts. He was not only an activist for Christ, but also an enforcer of the rights given by God directly to the nation's worthy citizens.

What I find distinct in Gregory's expression was the way in which the gun had become a necessary element in his political Scripture. Not that the gun wasn't sitting comfortably behind the actions of many of our early religious savants. "Onward, Christian soldiers" is an old refrain. The history of Brigham Young and his use of militias in Utah and Nevada demonstrates the militant and violent actions that can be used by religious sects. But for Gregory, the gun and the issue of gun rights had melded perfectly with a militant piety that fused the Ten Commandments with the first ten amendments to the Constitution, the Bill of Rights. Gun rights and God had found a perfect rhetorical alignment in his imagination. The psychic investment in guns had a sacred legitimation.

In Gregory's world, the gun and the rights associated with gun ownership renewed the original vision of God and the founding fathers, making the world orderly and free again. In many ways, conservatives in the twenty-first century needed gun rights as part of their political movement precisely because in the last fifty years they have been challenged directly by social movements that question the basic tenets of their political and religious positions. Their vision of the nation was at risk.[9]

Over the last half of the twentieth century, the social gospel of Christianity, mass nonviolent Christian activism, liberation theology, and myriad religious thinkers like Reinhold Niebuhr, Martin Luther King, Jr., and Gustavo Gutiérrez have all leveled scathing critiques against the social, economic, and legal injustices under United States capitalism, racism, and imperialism. These have coincided with secular challenges from civil-rights, feminist, and gay and lesbian activists to the traditional alignment of power in the community, the family, and marriage. Millions of Americans reacted to these movements with dismay, fearing not only that their country was under assault by liberal subversives, but also that their souls were in jeopardy.

In the spring of 2004, I attended my second Christian prayer breakfast at the annual meeting of the National Rifle Association. Two years earlier I had sat at a round table of respectful listeners and learned how the carnage of 9/11 had sent shock waves through the conservative Christian community. That year I listened to Lt. Col. Brian Birdwell describe the trauma of the 9/11 attack on the Pentagon that left his body burnt but his soul embraced by Christ. In often-halting words, he spoke of his ordeal and the strength that his faith gave him to survive the searing pain of his burns. He held steadfast and healed, with a deep, abiding love of God and country. His wife moved the breakfast audience to tears when, in simple, vivid words, she described her husband's intense physical suffering. In their shared grief, his escape from death was "a miracle of God," the saving of a "soldier of Christ."

This first breakfast had been sponsored by the Christian Sportsmen's Fellowship, a group that sustained the Teddy Roosevelt tradition of ethics, conservation, and hunting, and infused them with a strong dose of Christian witnessing, piety, and patriotism. Steve Bartkowski, a former quarterback for the Atlanta Falcons, was a popular spokesman for the organization, as was General Joe Foss, marine, war ace, governor of South Dakota, first commissioner of the American Football League, president of the NRA, and leader of the Campus Crusade for Christ. At the breakfast, I was given a prayer pamphlet and an opportunity to receive a free New Testament covered in camouflage.

Two years later, the prayer breakfast had even more participants and was becoming a popular event at the annual meeting of the NRA. In the long line to get into the banquet hall, people traded stories about how difficult it was to get a concealed-weapons permit in their state. One man couldn't believe how easy it was to get the magic slip of paper in my home state of Washington. A police officer, he thought there should be at least some mandatory training or shooting on a gun range with a qualified instructor. Safety checks on guns might be a good idea too. He was a reasonable voice in a sea of extreme rhetoric about freedom. I wondered how he felt about the religious scene at the NRA, but the line started moving ahead, and we parted ways.

God and patriotism were great slogan sources for politicians and the NRA; the details about statutes, ordinances, and laws were another matter. I had to remind myself that rhetoric might move the group, but individuals mucked up the neat and tidy categories that politicians and lobbyists used to promote their causes.

This year, the breakfast was sponsored by the International

Fellowship of Christian Businessmen, who call themselves "men of destiny" who are "disturbed by the deterioration of Godly principles once considered absolutes in our system and society and feel responsible, as Christians and professional men, to bring forth change."[10] The banquet hall was a lively scene of men and women ready for a moment of worship before the rounds of meetings, conferences, and walks through the massive gun show. We gave thanks at the breakfast for the NRA and Jesus Christ and heard that the NRA was made up of "purpose-driven people."

Peter Enns, writer of patriotic songs, hymns, and poems, was present to talk and to sell his CD, *Majestic Eagle*, with songs entitled, "We Are A People of Faith," "Our America Is Blessed," "America! One Nation United," and "The Prayer of Our Nation." The songs were played loudly over the PA system, and the lyrics cheered about what was right with America. The attack on 9/11 was a wake-up call to those who had become prosperous and complacent. 9/11 brought them back to God. Songs like "Keep America Strong" evoked the old-fashioned jeremiad that saw catastrophe as a warning to backsliders. In "Prayer of Our Nation," freedom also rested on the "men and women taking a stand to keep evil forces out of our land." The messages were direct: renew the faith or you and your nation will be destroyed.

The keynote speaker on this morning was the former Apollo astronaut Charlie Duke. He pleaded that the United States become—or, as he would have it, return to its original state as—a Christian theocracy. An Air Force colonel, he had not been given peace by his voyage aboard Apollo 16. Only later, when he went through the ordeal of his wife's depression and his disintegrating marriage, did he hear the call of Jesus. At a Bible-study weekend, he began to ask, "Who is this man, Jesus?" He finally felt "free will," and he chose to believe. "I knew that I knew that I knew it was the truth." And then began an "insatiable desire to read the Bible."

He spoke with humor and charisma about his conversion and urged the audience to find freedom of religion, not freedom from religion. He referenced the Pilgrims, the New England Primer, the Declaration of Independence, Patrick Henry, and George Washington. The United States would somehow be perfect if "one nation under God" meant that Jesus had come into the hearts and souls of everyone from the president to the Congress, to the governors, to the states, to the schools, and to each individual in the United States. The nation under Jesus, at every level of government and education, became an ideal. He added the caveat that other Christians and nonbelievers would be granted "asylum" in his reborn United States.

Charlie Duke's address offered a spiritual vision for the pragmatic political organizing at the meetings held later in the day. At those, I heard the usual alarms about people trying to take guns away from law-abiding citizens, followed by "the fight for our rights is part of the eternal struggle of good and evil," requiring courage and endurance. There was celebration that the gun-rights movement was "part of mainstream America." NRA members were told that Congress is "scared of you." They were the "ground troops" for voter recruitment and identification. They needed to "instill in kids" the need to register to vote. Their mission in registering people to vote was "not charity." It was "not altruistic." It was "patriotic" to protect the Second Amendment and the goals of the National Rifle Association. Each person was urged to register five people, five "freedom-loving brethren." The world was divided between the gun-grabber and the patriotic American gun owner.

At the prayer breakfast, the topic of guns had not even come up. It didn't need to. The mix of armed conservatism with a strong dose of fundamental Christian doctrine sanctified the gun. Both speakers I had heard at the NRA prayer breakfasts came from a group of born-again military preachers, retired or active, who ministered to the needs of patriotic Americans in both the armed forces and the civilian world. Tested in the fires of 9/11, the outer reaches of space, or the battlegrounds of World War II or Vietnam or one of the two wars in Iraq, they never questioned the military destiny of the United States, its sublime technology, or its ultimate religious destiny. The gun in the hand of the private citizen was not only a backup weapon for this militant millennial vision; the gun in the hand of the private citizen was a vast reserve army of patriots ready to defend God and country.

12

GLOBAL GUN GRABBERS

The red-white-and-blue billboard in downtown Lewiston, Idaho, boldly announced GET US OUT! OF THE UNITED NATIONS. A few years ago, while I was buying batteries for my camera, I read the same sentiments on a drugstore window in Clarkston, Washington, a store with a bookstand packed with John Birch Society materials. Lewiston and Clarkston face each other across the Snake River, and some of their residents shared the same fear of a New World Order driven by the money and power of the United Nations. The billboard was part of a campaign by the John Birch Society that included starter kits with buttons, bumper stickers, a reprint of *Preventing a United Nations Global Tyranny*, and helpful suggestions for contacting and petitioning the United States Congress.

If you did not like the red-white-and-blue design, they of-

fered a new poster in an ominous red glow: THE UNITED NATIONS
WANTS TO TAKE YOUR GUN! and featured the sculpture in the
United Nations Visitor's Plaza of a revolver with its barrel tied in
a knot, pointing to the sky. Entitled "Non-Violence," this sculpture by Karl Fredrik Reutersward, a gift from the government
of Luxembourg, somehow confirmed that the United Nations
wanted each and every law-abiding American citizen's gun. The
threat from the UN was no longer abstract, based on reports of
American soldiers in distant lands refusing to salute their blue-
helmeted commander or obey their UN orders. As a global gun-
grabber, the UN's abuse of power had turned intimate, invading
the home to confiscate private firearms.

The tirade against the United Nations by the John Birch Society and other gun-rights organizations now permeates gun
culture in the United States. At a show in Illinois, I bought
William Norman Grigg's 2001 attack on the United Nations,
*Global Gun Grab: The United Nations Campaign to Disarm
Americans.*[1] A senior editor of *The New American* magazine, a
publication of the John Birch Society, Grigg had an I-told-you-
so attitude about how the United Nations had set about to disarm law-abiding American citizens and destroy the United States
in the process. The John Birch position is worth lingering over
because its antagonism to the United Nations clarifies how gun
rights are used to undermine progressive democratic practices,
especially human rights.

Founded in the late 1950s, the John Birch Society has held
a long-standing conviction that the UN was intent on building a
world government, advocating Socialist and Communistic beliefs antithetical to the American way of life.[2] The Birchers were
not alone. For more than half a century, conservatives and extremists have denounced the United Nations as the gateway to
godlessness, anarchy, and corruption. In the 1950s, the Wichita,

Kansas, evangelist and outspoken anti-Semite Gerald B. Winrod delivered fiery diatribes against the United Nations as a Tower of Babel. And today the condemnation and ridicule continue in the genre of Christian science fiction, at policy institutes, and through conservative publishing houses.[3]

In the 1950s, right-wing rage against the United Nations was fueled by the UN stand on human rights and its implications for exposing brutal racial inequality in the United States. Many on the right, and Southern Democrats in particular, feared any open discussion in the United States of human rights because of the apartheid conditions in the South. Reforms in civil rights, education, and economic opportunities were an anathema to many in the political system, even liberals intent on party unity. Consequently, human rights were facilely equated with the Soviet Union and its Socialist and Communist collaborators.[4]

The John Birch Society saw its political power peak in 1964 with the Barry Goldwater campaign for presidency of the United States. Its membership has since diminished but not disappeared, as I note every time I drive past the drugstore in downtown Clarkston. A struggling organization, usurped by the gains of conservatives during the 1970s and '80s—who did not want to be associated with the Birchers' racist and anti-Semitic baggage—they have latched on to the gun-rights issue and positioned themselves as the group that had foreseen the dangers of the UN from the start.[5]

In 1998, a series of actions by the Clinton administration would create a common anti-UN bond between the John Birch Society and conservative gun-rights groups like the Second Amendment Foundation, the Gun Owners of America, and the NRA. The trouble started when the Clinton administration supported a UN resolution to limit illicit trafficking in firearms.

In the Second Amendment Foundation's Gottlieb-Tartaro Report of May, 1998, the two writers lashed out against Clinton and the UN, stating that "the resolution has little to do with enforcing current anti-smuggling measures on illegal firearms, but urges nations to tighten laws on international firearms sales. In other words, it's about new laws and global gun control. This is the first time the United States has endorsed a U. N. resolution on firearms regulation, an ominous sign."[6] These words struck a deep chord in the gun-rights world. A new enemy tactic had emerged to fight gun rights. Painted as the foe of gun owners for his entire time in office, President Bill Clinton was also said to want not only to use U.S. laws to take guns from law-abiding citizens, but to support the UN efforts to seize firearms. In 1997, the UN Crime Prevention and Criminal Justice Division, a body formed to draft resolutions for action by the UN Economic and Social Council, started to study international firearms regulations.[7] In 1998, at the Birmingham G8 Summit, the G8 nations—namely, Canada, France, Germany, Italy, Japan, Russia, the United Kingdom, and the United States—supported the UN efforts to create international guidelines to address the illicit trade. Since 1995, according to Project Ploughshares, the economic and social costs of crime, especially crime that crosses national borders, has become a top concern of G8 nations, and illicit weapons trafficking had become a G8 priority.[8]

In 1998, there were also diplomatic discussions about the lethal nature of global conflicts caused by small arms and light weapons (SALW), especially in African states.[9] In a speech to the UN Security Council Ministerial on Africa, Secretary of State Madeleine K. Albright affirmed the approach of African organizations such as Economic Community of Western African States (ECOWAS) and the Organization of African Unity to place a "moratorium on the manufacture and trade in small arms proposed by a group of West African nations."[10]

Though the hard realities of international crime were driving some of these initiatives, human security and the lethal violence to civilians in conflicts throughout the globe added to the discussions about illicit firearms trafficking. Concerns over the level of violence inflicted on civilians—especially women and children—by small arms and light weapons brought more than 150 nongovernmental organizations (NGOs) focused on civil society, humanitarian aid, human rights and women's rights to the UN conference.[11] During this period, the United Nations began to look beyond its traditional preoccupation with weapons of mass destruction (specifically nuclear, chemical, and biological weapons) to SALW traffic. And they began to raise pointed questions about human security, not only national security. When they did, the UN ran into American conservatives' effective use of the gun issue to bolster their cause.

A longtime opponent of the UN and supporter of the NRA, Jesse Helms was chairman of the Senate Foreign Relations Committee from 1995 to 2001. In 1999, he blocked efforts by the Clinton administration to support the West African moratorium on arms, stating in a letter to the U.S. Agency for International Development that the small-arms moratorium "proposes using U. S. taxpayers' money (among other things) to lobby or promote policies in foreign countries that may very well be a violation of the second amendment to the U. S. Constitution—if the federal government attempted such activities here at home."[12] This criticism of the United Nations as an organization that might trample on the Bill of Rights reinforced the supposed illegitimacy of many United Nations actions, especially those connected with multilateral peacekeeping, arms regulation, environmental justice, population control, and women's rights.[13]

In 2001, after George W. Bush's inauguration as president, the United Nations held its first Conference on Small Arms and Light Weapons, asking for international cooperation on controlling their illicit trafficking. By that time, the mounting attacks on the United Nations that had started during the Clinton administration had reached from the grassroots-level organizations like my John Birch Society neighbors at the Clarkston drugstore to the highest levels of government, including members of the Departments of State and Justice. Gun-rights organizations throughout the United States, and their defenders in Congress, joined in the chorus of outrage against the loss of American sovereignty and the dangers of multilateralism through the violation of Second Amendment rights.

As Bush's undersecretary of state for arms control and international security affairs, John R. Bolton was a strong supporter of unilateralism and the gun policies of Jesse Helms. Addressing the UN Conference on July 9, 2001, Bolton quoted from then-U.S. Attorney General John Ashcroft's interpretation of the Second Amendment. In fact, he quoted the very words that Ashcroft had written two months earlier, in one of his first acts as attorney general, in a letter to James Jay Baker, the executive director of the National Rifle Association's Institute for Legislative Action. "Just as the First and Fourth Amendments secure individual rights of speech and security respectively, the Second Amendment protects an individual right to keep and bear arms."[14]

To an amazed audience, Bolton revised the United Nations definition of "small arms" to include only what he labeled "military" weapons. Small arms would exclude hunting rifles and pistols and only include "strictly military arms—automatic rifles, machine guns, shoulder-fired missiles and rocket systems, light mortars." Citing our "cultural tradition of hunting and sport shooting," Bolton placed obstacles in the way of international monitoring of any individual government's role in arms transfer, since the definition of what constituted "hunting rifles and pistols" has been the subject of endless debate in the United States.[15] Even though the United States has put in place several strong controls over government-to-government transfer of arms and commercial sales, it joined with China and Russia at the UN's SALW Conference in sidestepping additional oversight of its own commercial or governmental role in the proliferation of arms throughout the world, especially surplus and recycled arms from areas of conflict previously involving United States military actions or arms support; what is called the "gray market" in gun trafficking.[16]

Bolton's message to the United Nations, evoking the Second Amendment, made it clear to conservatives that he could and would stand up to the UN. Overnight, Bolton became a veritable folk hero to the gun-rights world, and four years later, he became the controversial UN Ambassador-designate of George W. Bush's second administration, eventually sidestepping his Senate confirmation by receiving a direct presidential appointment in August, 2005. A link between gun rights and specific initiatives of the United Nations had been created, and a new political strategy to limit cooperation between the United Nations and the United States had been launched.

But to the adamant believer in the global gun grab, Bolton had danced with the devil simply by showing up and participating in the United Nations Conference. Grigg, writing in *The Global Gun Grab*, skewered Bolton and the NRA for getting involved in the bureaucratic machinations and manipulations of the United Nations at all. Previous to the conference, the National Rifle Association's Institute of Legislative Action (NRA–ILA) was accredited as an NGO and sent representatives to the conference. Grigg labeled such involvement as a weak "defensive strategy," since only complete withdrawal from the United Nations can work to stop its clear and present danger to the sovereignty of the United States.

The views of conservatives like John Bolton and Jesse Helms were part of a long-standing antipathy to the actions of the United Nations that had fermented amongst conservatives as they built their power base in the United States. Some of these objections can be clearly traced to Ronald Reagan's battle against the United Nations Educational, Scientific, and Cultural Organization (UNESCO) in the 1980s. Reagan stopped U.S. funding for UNESCO in 1984, citing financial mismanagement and his disagreement with its anti-Americanism, and in 1986 he defunded the United Nations Population Fund.[17] Conservatives had long objected to UNESCO's programs on the media, but these objections rarely touched on the potent matter of gun rights.

Even though George W. Bush returned the United States to UNESCO, other programs within the United Nations—notably the UN Population Fund (UNFPA)—remained controversial and underfunded by the United States. Other more recent efforts took aim at UN environmental, health, peacekeeping, and cultural initiatives. In 2003, in the latest in a series of conservative efforts to force a wedge between the United States and the UN, United States Representative Ron Paul of Texas introduced the "American Sovereignty Restoration Act" to "terminate U.S. participation in the United Nations."[18] That same year, in a speech before the U.S. House of Representatives, Paul introduced the "Right to Keep and Bear Arms Act," accusing the UN of fostering a "global regime of gun control."[19]

The depiction of the United Nations as global gun-grabber has clearly fed into preexisting fears of the organization on the radical Right. The UN now seemed to threaten the average American gun owner through international laws and cultural programs. What Grigg objected to most about the United Nations was its efforts at "psychological disarmament," and he particularly disliked UNESCO's efforts to promote a "culture of peace" through its educational programs.[20] Under the UNESCO women's agenda for a culture of peace, human security rests upon the foundation of human rights, not gun ownership.[21] Here began the slippery slope to worldwide disaster. "In recent years, since 'micro-disarmament' became an overt priority for the United Nations, efforts to 'demilitarize' the minds of people worldwide have proliferated." Grigg singled out the Commission on Global Governance and The Hague Appeal for their references to "norms of non-possession" of weapons to advance a culture of peace. This psychological disarmament involves demonizing "guns as intrinsically evil" and supporting "buy-backs" or "turn-ins" that could lead to "more aggressive confiscation programs."[22]

On a global level, we are in a period not dissimilar to what we faced in the 1970s, when gun rights began to trump civil rights as an effective political tool, undermining the social, economic, and political changes necessary for a democratic society. The insistence by a range of civil-rights groups that governing bodies, on city, county, state, and federal levels needed to uphold just laws, guaranteeing legal and political rights for all citizens, changed American race politics, bringing new powers to the federal government to enforce those rights in states, counties, and municipalities. Jim Crow laws in the South and their equivalent social and political counterparts in the North were struck down or altered only after a long process during the

1950s and '60s that was often hindered by violent means. But for many Americans economic change has lagged far behind, as has access to education, health care, home ownership, and secure neighborhoods. Similarly, campaigns for human rights, conducted by thousands of civil, humanitarian, and government agencies, have now run up against the renewed vigor of conservatives in the United States who have seized upon the old strategy of gun rights to hamper the necessary economic, social, and political changes that must accompany any meaningful solution to the problem of violence in the world.

For conservatives like Grigg, "psychological disarmament" of the sort practiced by the United Nations and its associates had already infiltrated the American mind with organizations like the "Million Mom March," which protested the proliferation of and access to guns in the inner city and sought clear restrictions on gun sales in the United States. For Grigg, physical force must remain in the hands of law-abiding American citizens to ward off the propaganda machine of the United Nations.[23] Without the gun, the American way would disappear.

The gun-rights movement and the political interpretation of the Second Amendment by conservatives have been used to resist social, political, and economic change beneficial to women and minorities in the United States and to marginalized people living throughout the developing world, particularly in Africa and South America. Globally, women and people of color looking to the UN for support have found themselves fighting directly against gun-rights organizations in the United States. In Brazil and Canada, women's organizations such as *Instituto Sou da Paz, Via Rio*, the National Association of Women and the Law, and

the YWCA of Canada have actively campaigned for gun regulation and have tried to stop the easing of these rules. In opposition, the NRA has sent advisors and ad campaigns to these
countries at strategic legislative moments, to either block new
legislation or restrict current regulations.[24]

On October 12, 2004, Wayne LaPierre, the executive vice
president of the NRA, debated Rebecca Peters from the International Action Network on Small Arms (IANSA) at Kings College in London over the role of the UN in the regulation of
firearms. Through IANSA and the UN, Peters coordinates the
efforts of some 600 international human rights, public health,
victim-support, and women's groups intent on curbing the proliferation of small arms in the world, especially in the developing world. Through the NRA, Wayne LaPierre has attempted to
prevent these UN initiatives, and Rebecca Peters, from formu-
lating international norms and regulations on small arms.

During the debate, Peters discussed armed conflict in places
like Congo and Sudan and the public and personal cost of such
gun violence. In contrast, LaPierre focused on how gun ownership was a fundamental right for Americans guaranteed them by
the Bill of Rights. He took the position of an advocate for the
victim, who must defend his or her life against predators invading their homes with intent to burglarize, rape, and kill. In support of his cause, LaPierre appealed directly to women and their
fear of rape. At one point, he held up a poster of an ad he had
designed for the NRA twenty years earlier that showed a distorted male face covered by what seemed to be a nylon stocking.
The poster contained the following question: "Should you shoot
a rapist before he cuts your throat?" He turned to Peters and asked
her that question, and then he announced that Peters would
disarm "the woman being attacked by this guy." Peters responded by saying, "Women need to live in societies that re-

spect their human rights. Women need to be protected by police forces, by judiciaries, by criminal justice systems. People who have guns for self-defense are not safer than people who don't."

As the debate continued, LaPierre painted the UN as no better than the ominous rapist intent on murder. Peters and the UN were part of a "new gargantuan global bureaucracy." Her activism was "some of the old socialist imaginings of the twentieth century." He talked about "global socialism" and its "colossal failure." Peters' words, like the UN's, were "empty promises."

In a slick use of sexist imagery, LaPierre called Peters an "international global nanny" and a "global godmother." In other words, her form of protection was useless; a nanny who cares for children has no power to protect by definition. A substitute mother, the global nanny, isn't even given the status of a mother. LaPierre demeaned and trivialized both Peters and the domestic work of many poor women by showing how powerless they were. As a "global godmother," Peters was even worse in LaPierre's eyes. She was misleading the innocent with her empty promises. Her beliefs appealed only to a child's fantasy. And she led the sheep to their slaughter.

"Trust in the gun" and "trust the Second Amendment" were phrases thrown at Peters as the sacred means of security. LaPierre accused Peters of not "liking our Bill of Rights" and coddling criminals. Again, she was cast as the weak woman whose compassion was the problem, the coddler who loves blindly, unwilling to discipline or punish.

To stave off these accusations, Peters spoke about the need for global human rights and cited the UN position that "governments have an obligation to protect the human rights of their citizens by restricting the proliferation of small arms." She spoke of government corruption, the arms race between police and criminals, and the public health and human cost of armed conflict zones in the world.

But LaPierre kept attacking Peters and, through her, the UN and human rights. Ultimately the UN was described as a failure, a fantasy, a form of "social engineering" that seduced "students on campus, journalists in the media, and intellectuals in think tanks. Elitists who think they know better than us how to live our lives, how to spend our money, how to educate our children, how to protect our home." Peters and the UN were the global bogeymen and women who would steal the freedoms of Americans and confiscate each and every gun from each and every individual freedom-loving American, thereby denying them the basic human right of all—gun ownership.

Silenced in this confrontation between LaPierre and Peters was any serious discussion of human rights and the recognition of the necessary social, political, and economic conditions that people need if they are to live and flourish in security. Similar to the period after World War II, when African Americans sought their human rights only to see what was left of their civil rights restricted by an alarmist conservative rhetoric of crime and punishment, human rights were again blindsided, but this time by a gun-rights advocate. The hard work of developing international regulations to stem global violence was trivialized into a right-to-carry gun policy for the world's citizens. The antidote to the harsh realities of peoples living in armed conflicts and under repressive regimes was a glib solution of providing more weapons for individual self-defense. Human rights were reduced to an expanded global arms trade.

Like a cowboy on a dusty Western street, the law-abiding American gun owner played his part in this debate as the citizen hero, a crime-stopper, a vigilante for justice, keeping the peace in a world unable to establish civil institutions, democratic practices, or economic justice. Gun rights and the Second Amendment had become major weapons used to renew the attack on the UN and to defend the interests of a few against the needs of marginalized peoples throughout the world and in the United States who need the protection of law and government to work, to vote, and to live in hope and peace.

AFTERWORD: LETHAL POLITICS

The United States floats in a sea of guns. Private citizens, police, federal and state agencies, and the military are armed to the teeth. The conservative gun-rights movement made acceptable to ordinary Americans a sanguine belief in lethal force to protect individuals from many disturbing social realities. This militarization of the American mind had roots in the rise of a state masculinity that found popular and political voice at the end of the nineteenth century. Strong white men armed with archaic power to conquer western lands, and their partners, disciplined white men with economic power, joined to rule the developing United States. Buffalo Bill and the American rifleman needed each other to create a national masculinity prepared and poised to exert national and imperial control.

As a people forged in the ethos of white nationalism, many

of us have loved the gun guys for more than a century. But this attachment to violence has meant that we must perform a moral charade. As a nation, we continually need to justify how and why we use the gun, only to pretend that we do not know the gun functions to further racial repression, economic disparity, and war. We search for moral reasons for our violence, unwilling simply to believe that we have placed too much trust in lethal force.

Since the 1970s, this psychic investment in guns has cast a criminal net over our social and economic lives. White privilege was challenged on a national level through the civil-rights movement, and the ethos of white nationalism responded by crying wolf. White victimhood needed the gun to conserve its power in social relations and the economy. The current use of the Second Amendment not only reassures individuals about personal security, but also reminds (typically white) citizens of the clear and present dangers from criminals and political enemies. Not only did we arm ourselves, but we also armed everyone in the government that represented us to fight a war against drugs, crime, and terror, until we mirrored back to each other our thoroughly militarized minds. Each soldier and citizen became an army of one.

Those labeled "liberal" or, worse, "socialist" or "Communist," who supposedly sought to control guns only buttressed the need for this national fantasy of force. To prohibit the gun would only increase the desire to violate the prohibition. If someone threatened to regulate guns, the voices raised against regulation only became louder. The force of fantasy and the fantasy of force have undermined public debate over the needed balance between individual and public interests and the use of lethal force by either citizens or the state. Instead, the gun-rights movement has rendered trivial the role government must play to provide human security through means other than force.

The semantic excess found in the gun-rights movement, which virtually screams about domestic terrorists such as librarians, schoolteachers, doctors, lawyers, and now global human-rights organizers who want gun-free zones and regulations, only shows us how far we are willing to impose our national fantasy on the world. Civil- and human-rights organizations that engage in social change are silenced by the conservative voice of the Second Amendment. This use of a legal and political amendment about the state-sanctioned use of force among citizens, individual states, and a national government to foster republican values has been turned against its citizens.

The Second Amendment has become a political weapon to stop the democratic processes set in motion during the eighteenth century. Those energies meant to engage in the building of civil government, and the participation of the people in the rights, privileges, and protections that such a government might provide, have been blindsided by a powerful lobby that keeps our eyes on crime and off what we must do to establish a just society. It is not a coincidence that the NRA has stood against federal elections reform. The conservative movement pushes for unfettered capitalism without allowing for the social benefits of wealth needed to provide basic care and economic opportunities for the nation's citizens. The gun protects the interests of a rabid capitalism while pointing its barrel at the criminal on the streets of poor neighborhoods.

Those who stand behind the gun have in effect broken the social compact to build a government that provides human security for its country's citizens. Those who stand behind the gun are too willing to align themselves with the militarization of the police and the massive defense budgets that we support to keep ourselves free. The gun speaks with a loud political voice that uses the reassurance of physical force to assuage our nagging cultural anxieties: we promote a lethal politics to let us sleep at night.

How much easier it is to believe in the politics of the gun, and to fight for our right to be armed, than to step in front of the gun and build social and civil institutions that sustain our society and promote economic and political justice. The gun is ultimately a shortcut, a strategy to sidestep consent. Our will to engage in democracy is what is at stake. The question remains: Can we put aside the lethal politics of the gun and take up again the challenge of democracy?

NOTES

Introduction

1. "The Power 25," *Fortune*, May 28, 2001.
2. For a detailed discussion of the ways in which women have entered contemporary gun debates, see Deborah Homsher, *Women & Guns: Politics and the Culture of Firearms in America* (Armonk, NY: M. E. Sharpe, 2001).
3. During the course of this project, I did have conversations with African American, Native American, Latino, and Asian American men about gun ownership and gun rights. Still, their numbers were small in comparison to those of white men. In fact, at one meeting I attended at the NRA annual convention in 2002, several men of color complained about the "white bright" membership of the NRA. Some were into the talk of gun politics; others saw them as a means for white men to hold onto their power, even if it was only the symbol of power attained by owning a gun kept in the closet. And a few insisted on the hardcore need for parity. If white men had guns, men of color better have guns, particularly for self-defense, an arms race percolating in the maze of race relations, one with a long history in Indian wars, slavery, and the post–Civil War South.
4. 1999 National Gun Policy Survey conducted by the National Opinion Research Center, University of Chicago, July 2000. I would add, however, that there is a continuous debate about whether women are buying a higher percentage of guns than in the past, especially in specific communities such as suburbs. See also Homsher, *Women & Guns.*
5. My approach to nationalism, national identities, and nation building has developed from the writings of Benedict Anderson, *Imagined Communities: Reflections on the Origin and Spread of Nationalism* (London: Verso, 1991); and Nira Yuval-Davis, *Gender and Nation* (London: Sage Publications, 1997).
6. Philip J. Cook and Jens Ludwig, *Guns in America: National Survey on Private Ownership and Use of Firearms* (Washington, DC: U.S. Department of Justice, Office of Justice Programs, National Institute of Justice, 1997).

7. William Hosley, *Colt: The Making of a Legend* (Amherst: University of Massachusetts Press, 1996), pp. 66–97.

8. Federal contracts dominated arms manufacturing before the Civil War, but gradually civilian markets emerged, gaining in strength after the war, especially in relation to sporting arms. Besides Hosley, see Harold F. Williamson, *Winchester: The Gun That Won the West* (New York: A. S. Barnes and Co., Inc., 1952); and Felicia Deyrup, *Arms Makers of the Connecticut Valley: A Regional Study of the Economic Development of the Small Arms Industry, 1798–1870* (Northampton, MA: Smith College Studies in History, v. 33, 1948), pp. 208–16.

1. Buffalo Bill at the Gun Show

1. Writings on the history of railroads in the United States are massive. For a recent introductory study see A. J. Veenendaal, *American Railroads in the Nineteenth Century* (Westport, CT: Greenwood Press, 2003). Individual rail lines often have historical societies connected to them. For the Rock Island, see the online site managed by the Rock Island Technical Society: http://storm.simpson.edu/~RITS, last accessed on July 26, 2005.

2. Alfred Dupont Chandler, ed., *The Railroads: The Nation's First Big Business: Sources and Readings* (New York: Harcourt, Brace & World, 1965); Sarah Gordon, *Passage to Union: How the Railroads Transformed American Life, 1829–1929* (Chicago: Ivan R. Dee, 1996); Maury Klein, *The Life and Legend of Jay Gould* (Baltimore: Johns Hopkins University Press, 1986); and John F. Stover, *Iron Road to the West: American Railroads in the 1850s* (New York: Columbia University Press, 1978).

3. Richard White, *"It's Your Misfortune and None of My Own": A New History of the American West* (Norman: University of Oklahoma Press, 1991); and Clyde A. Milner, Carol A. O'Connor, and Martha A. Sandweiss, *The Oxford History of the American West* (New York: Oxford University Press, 1994).

4. Abigail A. Kohn, *Shooters: Myths and Realities of America's Gun Cultures* (New York: Oxford University Press, 2004), pp. 39–54 and 83–102.

5. Frank Winch, *Thrilling Lives of Buffalo Bill, Colonel Wm. F. Cody, Last of the Great Scouts and Pawnee Bill, Major Gordon W. Lillie (Pawnee Bill) White Chief of the Pawnees* (New York: S. L. Parsons & Co., Inc., 1911).

6. Useful cultural studies of Buffalo Bill Cody include Joy S. Kasson, *Buffalo Bill's Wild West: Celebrity, Memory, and Popular History* (New York: Hill and Wang, 2000); L. G. Moses, *Wild West Shows and the Images of*

American Indians 1883–1933 (Albuquerque: University of New Mexico Press, 1996); and Paul Reddin, *Wild West Shows* (Urbana: University of Illinois Press, 1999).

7. William F. Cody, *The Life of Hon. William F. Cody, Known as Buffalo Bill, the Famous Hunter, Scout, and Guide: An Autobiography* (Lincoln: University of Nebraska Press, 1978), p. 41.

8. See the essay "Reading the West: Cultural and Historical Background," in Bill Brown, ed., *Reading the West: An Anthology of Dime Westerns* (Boston: Bedford Books, 1997), pp. 1–40; and Christine Bold, *Selling the Wild West: Popular Fiction, 1860–1960* (Bloomington: Indiana University Press, 1987). I am also indebted to the extensive historical research Richard Slotkin has done on myths of violence in the United States, and in particular his work, *The Fatal Environment: The Myth of the Frontier in the Age of Industrialization, 1800–1890* (Middletown, CT: Wesleyan University Press, 1985).

9. Sarah Watts, *Rough Rider in the White House: Theodore Roosevelt and the Politics of Desire* (Chicago: University of Chicago Press, 2003), pp. 56–73.

10. In his autobiography, Cody ridiculed Mexicans and freed slaves, especially black men known as buffalo soldiers, who served in the army on the frontier. For a discussion of buffalo soldiers, see Quintard Taylor, *In Search of the Racial Frontier: African Americans in the American West, 1528–1990* (New York: W. W. Norton, 1998).

11. William Hosley, *Colt: The Making of a Legend* (Amherst: University of Massachusetts Press, 1996), pp. 66–97.

12. Ibid., p. 83.

13. Julian Somora, Joe Bernal, and Albert Peña, *Gunpowder Justice: A Reassessment of the Texas Rangers* (Notre Dame: University of Notre Dame Press, 1979), pp. 10–45.

14. The mass production of firearms parallels the development of industrial tool and machine manufacturing in the United States. For the transformation of production, especially the conflicts between semiskilled and skilled labor, see David A. Zonderman, *Aspirations and Anxieties: New England Workers and the Mechanized Factory System, 1815–1859* (New York: Oxford University Press, 1992), pp. 53–62.

15. David F. Burg, *Chicago's White City of 1893* (Lexington: University Press of Kentucky, 1976).

16. R. L. Wilson and Greg Martin, *Buffalo Bill's Wild West: An American Legend* (New York: Random House, 1998), p. 68.

17. Harold F. Williamson, *Winchester: The Gun That Won the West* (New York: A. S. Barnes and Co., Inc., 1952), pp. 185–88.

18. See the online site of the Buffalo Bill Historical Society at http://www .bbhc.org, last accessed on July 26, 2005.

19. Larry McMurtry, *The Colonel and Little Missie: Buffalo Bill, Annie Oakley, and the Beginnings of Superstardom in America* (New York: Simon & Schuster, 2005), p. 5.

20. The term "fetish" was originally used in the study of religion, especially the study by Europeans of religions in Africa and Egypt. In the nineteenth century, both Karl Marx and Sigmund Freud used the term "fetish" to identify symptoms of the psyche and the political economy, respectively. For Freud, the fetish was illogical and resolved the conflict for the son of the mother's lack of a penis. The fetish was a substitute for the maternal penis that made the fear of castration controllable and the sexual pleasure derived from women possible, hence it was a protection against both castration and homosexuality. With Marx, commodities acted like fetishes in that they seemed to convey life while hiding their means of production based on human labor. The social character of labor that establishes relations between humans assumes the form of a relation between things. Hence, the utility of a commodity is not mysterious, but its value is, needing interpretation to uncover its system of production and exchange and its dependence upon social processes. Sigmund Freud, *The Standard Edition of the Complete Psychological Works of Sigmund Freud*, vol. 22 (London: Hogarth Press, 1964), pp. 149–57; David McLellan, ed., *Karl Marx: Selected Writings* (New York: Oxford University Press, 2000), pp. 472–80. See also William Pietz, "The Fetish of Civilization: Sacrificial Blood and Monetary Debt," in Peter Pels and Oscar Salemink, eds., *Colonial Subjects: Essays on the Practical History of Anthropology* (Ann Arbor: University of Michigan Press, 1999).

21. Though as Janice Radway points out in *Reading the Romance: Women, Patriarchy, and Popular Literature* (Chapel Hill: University of North Carolina Press, 1991), there is an implied cultural threat in the form of protection provided by the romance novel.

22. See Benedict Anderson, *Imagined Communities: Reflections on the Origin and Spread of Nationalism* (London: Verso, 1991); and Nira Yuval-Davis, *Gender and Nation* (London: Sage Publications, 1997).

2. Rebirth of a Nation

1. The extent to which free and enslaved blacks were permitted access to and ownership of firearms varied from state to state. Clearly, before the Revolutionary War, slaves were used to fight in specific colonial cam-

paigns against native peoples, especially the Yamasee War (1715–16). After the Revolution, the Militia Act of 1792 specified that "each and every free able-bodied white male citizen" between the ages of eighteen and forty-five must enroll in a state militia. Whiteness was a critical designation in the Act, but the practice of raising and training militiamen was under local control and subject to the political, racist, and economic needs of each state and region. The African American ownership of firearms for personal protection was also caught in the legal and political contradictions of slave labor, slave insurrections, and racist fear of African Americans by both Northern and Southern whites. See A. Leon Higginbotham Jr., *In the Matter of Color: The Colonial Period* (New York: Oxford University Press, 1978); and Alan Gallay, *The Indian Slave Trade: The Rise of English Empire in the American South, 1670–1717* (New Haven, CT: Yale University Press, 2002). For an important discussion of how the cultural concept of "whiteness" became a crucial part of the legal, political, and social system in the United States, see Matthew Frye Jacobson, *Whiteness of a Different Color: European Immigrants and the Alchemy of Race* (Cambridge, MA: Harvard University Press, 1998); Gary B. Nash, *Forging Freedom: The Formation of Philadelphia's Black Community, 1720–1840* (Cambridge, MA: Harvard University Press, 1988); and Stephen Kantrowitz, *Ben Tillman & the Reconstruction of White Supremacy* (Chapel Hill: University of North Carolina Press, 2000). For an example of a legal discussion of the relationship between race and firearms ownership that has been reduced to the single issue of self-defense in face of a civil government that has historically been unwilling to protect black citizens, see Robert J. Cottrol and Raymond T. Diamond, "The Second Amendment: Toward an Afro-Americanist Reconsideration," *Journal of Firearms and Public Policy* 7 (1995): 75–111.

2. My discussion of the Reconstruction is drawn from W. E. B. DuBois, *Black Reconstruction in America* (New York: Russell & Russell, 1962, rpt. 1935); Eric Foner, *Reconstruction: America's Unfinished Revolution, 1863–1877* (New York: Harper & Row, 1988); and Leon Litwack, *Been in the Storm So Long: The Aftermath of Slavery* (New York: Knopf, 1979). See also Jonathan Birnbaum and Clarence Taylor, *Civil Rights since 1787: A Reader on the Black Struggle* (New York: New York University Press, 2000).

3. See, for his discussion of the disenfranchisement of freed blacks, Robert M. Goldman, *Reconstruction and Black Suffrage: Losing the Vote in Reese and Cruikshank* (Lawrence: University Press of Kansas, 2001), p. 141.

4. An early major decision on the Second Amendment came during the vio-

lence of Reconstruction. In *United States v. Cruikshank*, 92 U.S. 542 (1875), an ambiguous decision restricted the power of the federal government and reinforced the power of the state to interpret civil rights.

5. I am also indebted to Robert M. Goldman's excellent discussion of the Colfax Massacre in his *Reconstruction and Black Suffrage*, pp. 42–59, 108–43.

6. Ibid., p. 45.

7. Ibid.

8. For general discussions of the Ku Klux Klan and lynchings in the United States, see David M. Chalmers, *Hooded Americanism: The First Century of the Ku Klux Klan, 1865–1965* (Garden City, NY: Doubleday, 1965); Allen W. Release, *White Terror: The Ku Klux Klan Conspiracy and Southern Reconstruction* (Baton Rouge: Louisiana State University Press, 1971); and Philip Dray, *At the Hands of Persons Unknown: The Lynching of Black America* (New York: Random House, 2002).

9. See in particular the discussion of Leon Litwack in *Been in the Storm So Long*.

10. Otis A. Singletary, *Negro Militia and Reconstruction* (Austin: University of Texas Press, 1957), p. vii.

11. Ibid., pp. 129–44.

12. Ibid., p. 131.

13. Ibid., p. 137.

14. Ibid., p. 139.

15. Ibid., p. 143.

16. In *Reports of Committees of the House of Representatives for the Second Session of the Forty-Second Congress 1871–72* (Washington, DC: Government Printing Office, 1872), there are instances of reprisals against white women for teaching in Freedman Bureau schools, running distilleries or restaurants where black men gathered, permitting black men to buy sex or to socialize in mixed-racial groups. White women were beaten, forced out of their communities, and in two instances ritually mutilated by having their pubic hair burned. *The Birth of a Nation* also contributed to the rise of what is called the second Klan; see Nancy MacLean, *Behind the Mask of Chivalry: The Making of the Second Ku Klux Klan* (New York: Oxford University Press, 1994). For a discussion of how the black rapist became a popular image in both the North and South in the late nineteenth century, see Gail Bederman, *Manliness & Civilization: A Cultural History of Gender and Race in the United States, 1880–1917* (Chicago: University of Chicago Press, 1995), especially her chapter on Ida B. Wells.

17. In their efforts to stem irresponsible access to firearms in the United States, the NAACP initiated a lawsuit in 1999 against a long list of arms manufacturers. They lost.

18. Henry Levy, "CORE's Martin Luther King Jr. Annual Awards Dinner," *Jewish Post,* online version, http://www.jewishpost.com, last accessed on July 27, 2005.

19. Frank R. Parker, *Black Votes Count: Political Empowerment in Mississippi after 1965* (Chapel Hill: University of North Carolina Press, 1990), pp. 198–209.

3. The Rifle Fraternity

1. Jeremy Black, in *Warfare in the Western World, 1882–1975* (Bloomington: Indiana University Press, 2002), discusses how important culture and ideology were to the aims of an imperialism that used military force (p. 3). See also Graham A. Cosmas, *An Army for Empire: The United States Army in the Spanish-American War* (Shippensburg, PA: White Mane Pub. Co., 1994); and Gerald F. Linderman, *The Mirror of War: American Society and the Spanish-American War* (Ann Arbor: University of Michigan Press, 1974).

2. To understand the history of the state militias as they changed into what would become the National Guard, see Jerry Cooper, *The Rise of the National Guard: The Evolution of the American Militia, 1865–1920* (Lincoln: University of Nebraska Press, 1997), pp. 65–107. For an earlier history of the colonial and eighteenth-century militias, see Lawrence Delbert Cress, *Citizens in Arms: The Army and the Militia in American Society to the War of 1812* (Chapel Hill: University of North Carolina Press, 1982). For an interesting essay on the connection between the concept of the citizen soldier and Republican ideology in relation to the Second Amendment, see David C. Williams, "Civic Republicanism and the Citizen Militia: The Terrifying Second Amendment," *Yale Law Journal* 101, no. 3 (1991): 551–615. For a differing approach, see Joyce Lee Malcolm, *To Keep and Bear Arms: The Origins of an Anglo-American Right* (Cambridge, MA: Harvard University Press, 1994). For the familial, racial, and economic conflicts shaping communal duty for citizen soldiers in the revolutionary period, see Robert A. Gross, *The Minutemen and Their World* (New York: Hill and Wang, 1976).

3. In this chapter, "state militia" only refers to volunteers and not the legal concept of the obligated militia, composed of white men between the ages of eighteen and forty-five, organized by the Militia Act of 1792 and

regulated by the states and the federal government through the Second Amendment of the United States Constitution with provisions for officers and training as directed in the Constitution.

4. H. Richard Uviller and William G. Merkel, *The Militia and the Right to Arms, or, How the Second Amendment Fell Silent* (Durham: Duke University Press, 2002), p. 125.

5. The complex legal and constitutional questions about how and when to use state militia units in foreign wars versus domestic conflict are discussed in Cooper, *The Rise of the National Guard*, pp. 128–72. Eventually, the state militias were brought under federal control through a series of federal actions, commencing in 1903 with the Dirk Act and followed by the National Defense Act of 1916.

6. See Herbert G. Gutman, *Work, Culture, and Society in Industrializing America: Essays in American Working-Class and Social History* (New York: Knopf, 1976). For a discussion of the emergence of the middle-class, see Olivier Zunz, *Making America Corporate, 1870–1920* (Chicago: University of Chicago Press, 1990).

7. How state militias were used in labor conflict varied from state to state. Some of the worst abuses occurred in Colorado and Pennsylvania. See George G. Suggs, *Colorado's War on Militant Unionism: James H. Peabody and the Western Federation of Miners* (Detroit: Wayne State University Press, 1972). For a defense of militia activity, see Cooper, *The Rise of the National Guard*, pp. 44–64. For an insider account, see Walter Merriam Pratt, *"The Tin Soldiers": The Organized Militia and What It Really Is* (Boston: Richard G. Badger, 1912).

8. The rise of fraternal clubs and a national concept of manhood are further explored by Mary Ann Clawson, *Constructing Brotherhood: Class, Gender, and Fraternalism* (Princeton, NJ: Princeton University Press, 1989); and Dana Nelson, *National Manhood: Capitalist Citizenship and the Imagined Fraternity of White Men* (Durham, NC: Duke University Press, 1998). For further studies on masculinity at the turn of the century, see J. A. Mangan and James Walvin, eds., *Manliness and Morality: Middle-Class Masculinity in Britain and America, 1800–1940* (New York: St. Martin's Press, 1987); and Anthony E. Rotundo, *American Manhood: Transformations in Masculinity from the Revolution to the Modern Era* (New York: Basic Books, 1993).

9. I am indebted to Michael A. Gordon's fine study, *The Orange Riots: Irish Political Violence in New York City* (Ithaca, NY: Cornell University Press, 1993).

10. Russell S. Gilmore, "'Another Branch of Manly Sport': American Rifle

Games, 1840–1900," in Jan E. Dizard, Robert Merrill Muth, and Stephen P. Andrews, Jr., eds., *Guns in America: A Reader* (New York: New York University Press, 1999), p. 108.

11. General George W. Wingate, *History of the Twenty-Second Regiment: National Guard of the State of New York, from Its Organization to 1895* (New York: Edwin W. Dayton, 1896), p. 425. For his approach to rifle practice, see his articles in *Army Navy Journal* 8, no. 47 and nos. 50–52 (July–August, 1871). Also, see his later articles, "The Development of the Modern Rifle" in *Arms and the Man* 59, nos. 3–7 (October–November, 1915).

12. Wingate, *History of the Twenty-Second Regiment*, p. 145.

13. An important example of the controversies of the times is found in the life of Colonel Frederick Funston of the 20th Kansas Infantry Regiment. For his combat role in the Philippines that left entire communities burnt to the ground and for his capture of Emilio Aguinaldo, the leader of the resistance movement to American control, he was made a public hero. But he was also attacked as a disgrace to American democratic ideals. Mark Twain wrote with biting satire about this model of masculinity in his "In Defense of General Funston," in Jim Zwick, ed., *Mark Twain's Weapons of Satire: Anti-Imperialist Writings on the Philippine-American War* (Syracuse: Syracuse University Press, 1992). See also Philip S. Foner and Richard C. Winchester, eds., *The Anti-Imperialist Reader: A Documentary History of Anti-Imperialism in the United States* (New York: Holmes & Meier, 1984).

14. The use of rifles in guerrilla and counter-insurgency tactics was certainly still necessary in European colonial wars and in Cuba and the Philippines. See Jeremy Black, *Warfare in the Western World*, p. 6.

15. Gilmore, "'Another Branch of Manly Sport,'" pp. 105–121. Gilmore also discusses the participation of German Americans in these sports.

16. In contrast, the average working-class family at the end of the nineteenth century might spend a nickel once a week to take a streetcar ride, buy a beer, or go to a dance hall, while a serious rifleman could buy special match rifles built specifically for shooting games. Kathy Peiss, *Cheap Amusements: Working Women and Leisure in Turn-of-the-Century New York* (Philadelphia: Temple University Press, 1986), pp. 34–55.

17. Annie Oakley also criticized how shooting clubs excluded women because the clubs were becoming places to drink rather than to practice the sober sport of rifle practice. "There are only a few shooting grounds I know of where any provision is made for lady visitors; besides, a majority of shooting clubs have barrooms attached, and very often part of the

small clubroom is used for the sale of beer and liquors." Annie Oakley, "Field Sports for Women," *Shooting and Fishing: A Journal of the Rifle, Gun, and Rod* 21, no. 9 (December 17, 1896): 188.

18. George W. Wingate, *Through the Yellowstone Park on Horseback* (Moscow: University of Idaho Press, 1999), pp. 32–33.

19. Anon., "In Memoriam: Arthur Corbin Gould," *Shooting and Fishing: A Journal of the Rifle, Gun, and Rod* 35, no. 11 (December 24, 1903): 223.

20. Anon., "Third Annual Sportsmen's Exposition" *Shooting and Fishing: A Journal of the Rifle, Gun, and Rod* 21, no. 22 (March 18, 1897): 445.

21. Sarah Watts, *Rough Rider in the White House: Theodore Roosevelt and the Politics of Desire* (Chicago: University of Chicago Press, 2003), pp. 123–92.

22. Theodore Roosevelt, *Ranch Life and the Hunting-Trail* (Ann Arbor: University Microfilms, Inc., 1966), p. 131.

23. Daniel Justin Herman, *Hunting and the American Imagination* (Washington, DC: Smithsonian Institution Press, 2001), pp. 173–87.

24. Quoted in Harold F. Williamson, *Winchester: The Gun That Won the West* (New York: A. S. Barnes and Co., Inc., 1952), pp. 199–200.

25. Anon., "The N.R.A. Has 'Border Troubles,'" *Arms and the Man* 40, no. 15 (July 6, 1916): 283. Since 1903, with the creation of the National Board for the Promotion of Rifle Practice, the National Rifle Association had been intimately involved with the building of rifle ranges for civilian use. Also, in 1905, surplus military firearms and ammunition could be sold at cost to civilian rifle clubs if they were sponsored by the National Rifle Association. As Osha Gray Davidson, in *The NRA and the Battle for Gun Control: An Expanded Edition* (Iowa City: University of Iowa Press, 1998), writes, these years were the "best of times for the NRA," p. 27. With surplus firearms also given free to these clubs and Congressional funding provided for shooting matches, the National Rifle Association had created a "lucrative monopoly for itself," p. 28.

26. Maury Klein, *Rainbow's End: The Crash of 1929* (New York: Oxford University Press, 2001).

27. See Clare Bond Potter, *War on Crime: Bandits, G-men, and the Politics of Mass Culture* (New Brunswick, NJ: Rutgers University Press, 1998); and Bryan Burrough, *Public Enemies: America's Greatest Crime Wave and the Birth of the FBI, 1933–34* (New York: Penguin, 2004).

28. *The American Rifleman* 85, no. 2 (February 1937): 44.

29. *The American Rifleman* 85, no. 7 (July 1937), "Powder Smoke" column.

30. Anon., "The Most Uncommon Thing," *The American Rifleman* 89, no. 3 (March, 1941): 4.

31. C. B. L., "Re-Dedication," *The American Rifleman* 89, no. 5 (May 1941): 4.

32. Anon., "Our Responsibility," *The American Rifleman* 89, no. 6 (June 1941): 4.

33. Anon., "Which Flag?" *The American Rifleman* 89, no. 7 (July 1941): 4.

34. Raymond J. Stan, "The N.R.A. and National Defense," *The American Rifleman* 89, no. 9 (September, 1941): 7.

35. Ibid., p. 8.

4. Start Shooting

1. Although a detailed analysis of the conflicts surrounding the Second Amendment goes beyond the scope of this book, certain key writings should be noted. The legal and historical debates about the Second Amendment have escalated since the 1960s. In his introduction to *The Second Amendment in Law and History: Historians and Constitutional Scholars on the Right to Bear Arms* (New York: The New Press, 2000), Carl T. Bogus wrote that the first legal article that promoted the individual rights interpretation was written by a student and published in the *William and Mary Law Review*. In its first source, the article cited the NRA's magazine, *American Rifleman*. Bogus then described the extent of the NRA's involvement in individual rights legal argumentation. Intense debates in the 1980s shaped much that had been articulated by historians on the Second Amendment. Saul Cornell located this modern historical debate as stemming from an essay by Robert Shalhope that reexamined colonial and revolutionary history, "The Ideological Origins of the Second Amendment," *Journal of American History* 64 (1982): 599–614. Shalhope's position was critiqued by Lawrence Delbert Cress in his essay, "An Armed Community: The Origins and Meanings of the Right to Bear Arms," *Journal of American History* 71 (1984): 22–42. For individual rights interpretations in particular see Sanford Levinson, "The Embarrassing Second Amendment," *Yale Law Journal* 99 (1989): 637–59; Eugene Volokh, "The Commonplace Second Amendment," *New York University Law Review* 73 (1998): 793–821; and Akil Reed Amar, *The Bill of Rights: Creation and Reconstruction* (New Haven, CT: Yale University Press, 1998), pp. 46–59. No agreement has been reached by lawyers or historians on how to interpret the Second Amendment, and the scholarship resulting from the disagreements over whether the amendment affirmed individual or collective rights has only intensified, with some scholars asking for analysis beyond these two categories into the concept of an individual civic right. See Saul Cornell, ed., *Whose Right to Bear*

Arms Did the Second Amendment Protect? (Boston: Bedford/St. Martin's Press, 2000). Also see H. Richard Uviller and William G. Merkel, *The Militia and the Right to Arms, Or, How the Second Amendment Fell Silent* (Durham, NC: Duke University Press, 2002) for an overview of legal and historical scholarship in relation to the transformation of the state militias.

2. As such, politics transforms legal language into ideology. In the process, cultural conflicts are often represented in absolute statements that attempt to resolve these conflicts but can never do so except by reproducing even more polarized ideological language. The semantic excess and belief in fundamental statements of truth in much ideology only underscore the disruptive nature of the conflicts they attempt to resolve. Legal language, in its quest for certainty beyond semantic ambiguity, often fails to account for not only the dynamic nature of cultural meanings but also the deep-seated and often obscure reasons hidden beneath static interpretations that seek authority in legal and historical experts.

3. David E. Young, *The Origin of the Second Amendment: A Documentary History of the Bill of Rights 1787–1792* (Ontonagon, MI: Golden Oak Books, 1995). This massive tome contains much to show how nervous our founders were about disciplining, training, and regulating citizen militias. But despite these concerns, the author argues for an armed populace ready to fight for liberty "free of government infringement," *lii.* For a good discussion of anti-Federalist writings, see Saul Cornell, *The Other Founders: Anti-Federalism and the Dissenting Tradition in America, 1788–1828* (Chapel Hill: University of North Carolina Press, 1999).

4. Confidential interview on October 1, 2003.

5. Robert A. Gross, *The Minutemen and Their World* (New York: Hill and Wang, 1976).

6. Leonard L. Richards, *Shay's Rebellion: The American Revolution's Final Battle* (Philadelphia: University of Pennsylvania Press, 2002).

7. For a fine essay about eighteenth-century language of social contract and universal military conscription and its relevance to contemporary defense policies, see Elaine Scarry, "War and the Social Contract: Nuclear Policy, Distribution, and the Right to Bear Arms," *University of Pennsylvania Law Review* 139, no. 5 (May 1991): 1257–316.

5. Reading *American Rifleman*

1. Daniel Justin Herman, *Hunting and the American Imagination* (Washington: Smithsonian Institution Press, 2001), pp. 271, 281, and footnotes 1 and 2 on pp. 346–47.

2. Confidential interview on September 29, 2005.

3. The history of the Ohio Gun Collectors Association can be found online at http://www.ocgca.com, last accessed on July 20, 2005.

4. Ibid.

5. James E. Serven, "Conducting the Gun Show," *The American Rifleman* 109, no. 6 (June 1961): 48

6. William J. Vizzard, in *Shots in the Dark: The Policy, Politics, and Symbolism of Gun Control* (New York: Rowman & Littlefield Publishers, Inc., 1997), writes that "As the gun market grew during the 1960s and 1970s, gun shows evolved from events for collectors to display and trade rare and unusual guns into swap meets for guns and associated items. Gun shows became magnets for unlicensed firearms dealers. Although many innocent transactions took place at these events, they provided cover for large-scale unlicensed dealers and provided an easy source of untraceable firearms for criminals and violent militants," p. 122. Also, the Gun Control Act of 1968 did not define accurately what was meant by "engaging in business," and attempts to clarify its meaning by defining who was a "dealer" ran into protests from collectors, large commercial sellers, and the gun lobby, pp. 122–25.

7. See Lee Clark Mitchell, *Westerns: Making the Man in Fiction and Film* (Chicago: University of Chicago Press, 1996); and my *Rodeo Queens and the American Dream* (New York: PublicAffairs, 2002).

8. See ad in *The American Rifleman* 109, no. 6 (June 1961): 75, of a "Colt Single Action Army," with the phrase "Still Blazing New Frontiers."

9. See ad in *The American Rifleman* 139, no. 10 (October 1991): 5 with "The Gun that Won the Westerns," and in the same issue see "John Wayne Western Commemoratives .45," p. 13.

10. In 1973, many of these issues were taken over by a new NRA publication, *The American Hunter.*

11. The Gun Control Act of 1968 has often been seen as the reason why gun politics heated up in the United States. Clearly, it altered the way in which commercial transactions involving firearms occurred, requiring a federal license to do business, but the nationalistic use of guns, with its valorization of a specific type of national manhood, also was threatened during the 1960s, and this context of cultural and social change is essential to an understanding of the controversies over guns during this period.

12. See Osha Gray Davidson, *Under Fire*, pp. 30–36.

13. Editorials, "The Right to Keep and Bear Arms," *The American Rifleman* 108, no. 4 (April 1960): 16 and "The Price of Individual Rights," *The American Rifleman* 108, no. 7 (July 1960): 16.

14. Editorial, "Consent of the Governed," *The American Rifleman* 109, no. 7 (July 1961): 16.

15. Bartlett Rummel, "To Have and Bear Arms," *The American Rifleman* 112, no. 6 (June 1964): 38–42.

16. See ad, *The American Rifleman* 112, no. 3 (March 1964), back of front cover.

17. *Report of the National Advisory Commission on Civil Disorders* (New York: The New York Times Co., 1968), p. 2.

18. Ibid., p. 18.

19. Editorial, *The American Rifleman* 116, no. 7 (July 1968): 16.

20. Ibid.

21. Tom Diaz, *Making a Killing: The Business of Guns in America* (New York: The New Press, 1999), pp. 21 and 68. Forty-six percent of guns available to civilians in the twentieth century were produced in the twenty years between 1974 and 1993. And in the last twenty years, "the gun industry has deliberately enhanced its profits by increasing the lethality—the killing power—of its products."

22. For instance, the Gun Control Act of 1968 restricted the import of cheap guns, called "Saturday Night Specials," often used as crime guns, though it stopped short of restricting its domestic production. Vizzard, *Shots in the Dark*, pp. 93–105.

23. Editorial, *The American Rifleman* 118, no. 2 (February 1970): 16.

24. Anon., "What They Heard," *The American Rifleman* 119, no. 6 (June 1971): 55.

25. Ibid.

26. *The American Rifleman* Staff, "NRA Directors Advocate Fair Firearms Laws," *The American Rifleman* 120, no. 1 (January 1972): 45.

27. Ashley Halsey, Jr., "Can the Second Amendment Survive?" *The American Rifleman* 121, no. 3 (March 1973): 17.

28. A 1973 article by Harold W. Glassen has become something of an embarrassment to the NRA today, because sections concluded that the Second Amendment "does not create the right of the people to keep and bear arms, but it prevents the Congress from infringing such right—thereby recognizing that such right exists." Not the United States Constitution, but British common law handed down the right through an argument about rights implied and not specifically stated. Such legalism and case-law complexities would create havoc for the conservatives in the NRA, who wanted a clear rallying cry. Subsequently, a moral, not a legal, argument about the Second Amendment followed Glassen's article. In a column next to his article, Edward Y. Breese simply asserted that "no one has

the ability or the authority to determine whether or not I am qualified to bear arms." Who cared that Glassen had just stated that the Second Amendment was "a slender reed upon which to rely"? Further, the armed citizen was hyped as a heroic crime-stopper. "If my neighbor is armed as I am, it causes me no fear. Indeed, I would feel safer if everyone on our block owned, understood, and was prepared to use a gun in our mutual defense. If this were the case, there would be no threat of armed robbery or riot in our area." See Harold W. Glassen, "Right to Bear Arms Is Older than the Second Amendment," *The American Rifleman* 121, no. 4 (April 1973): 22–23, and Edward Y. Breese's column next to Glassen's article.

29. See ad, *The American Rifleman* 124, no. 6 (June 1976): 12.

30. Josh Sugarmann, *National Rifle Association: Money, Firepower & Fear* (Washington, DC: National Press Books, 1992), pp. 45–65. See also the discussion of Harlon Carter's background, especially his killing of a young man, Ramon Casiano, in Laredo, Texas, in Osha Gray Davidson, *Under Fire*, pp. 31–34.

31. NRA Institute for Legislative Action Reports, "The Right to Keep and Bear Arms: An Analysis of the Second Amendment," *The American Rifleman* 125, no. 8 (August 1977): 38.

32. NRA Official Journal Insert, *The American Rifleman* 127, no. 5 (May 1979): 5.

33. Ibid.

6. Uncivil Rights

1. Confidential interview on January 14, 2004.

2. Gregory L. Schneider, ed., *Conservatism in America since 1930* (New York: New York University Press, 2003), pp. 211–30. See also Schneider's *Cadres for Conservatism: Young Americans for Freedom and the Rise of the Contemporary Right* (New York: New York University Press, 1999), pp. 31–54.

3. Ibid., p. 230.

4. John A. Andrew III, *The Other Side of the Sixties: Young Americans for Freedom and the Rise of Conservative Politics* (New Brunswick, NJ: Rutgers University Press, 1997), pp. 32–52.

5. An ad for the committee can be found in *The New Guard: The Magazine of Young Americans for Freedom* 14, no. 1 (March 1974), p. 33.

6. Larry Pratt, the controversial co-chair of Pat Buchanan's 1996 presidential campaign, co-founded Gun Owners of America in 1975 with H. L. Richardson.

7. Confidential interview on January 14, 2004.

8. For Nixon's part in the undermining of Muskie's bid for the Democratic nomination, see Anthony Summers, *The Arrogance of Power: The Secret World of Richard Nixon* (New York: Penguin Books, 2000), pp. 381–82; and Stanley I. Kutler, *Abuse of Power: The New Nixon Tapes* (New York: The Free Press, 1997), pp. 37–38, 40, and 454. For his attitude toward McGovern, see Summers, *The Arrogance of Power*, p. 402.

9. Eric P. Veblen, *The Manchester Union Leader in New Hampshire Elections* (Hanover, NH: The University Press of New England, 1975), pp. 1–20,

10. Even though Strom Thurmond did have conflicts with the Young Americans for Freedom (YAF), he supported many of its positions. The YAF constantly tried to redirect the charge of racism against its organization as one of liberals or Communists versus conservatives. Black power and black militancy were Communist-inspired, while the conservative panacea of individual initiative was color-blind.

11. Lyndon B. Johnson, "Special Message to the Congress: The American Promise," delivered March 15, 1965, to Congress, online at http://www.lbjlib.utexas.edu, last accessed on August 4, 2005.

12. Taylor Branch, *Parting the Waters: America in the King Years 1954–1963* (New York: Simon & Schuster, 1988), and his *Pillar of Fire: America in the King Years, 1963–65* (New York: Simon & Schuster, 1998). For a general overview, see Juan Williams, *Eyes on the Prize: America's Civil Rights Years* (New York: Penguin, 1988) and James M. Washington, ed., *A Testament of Hope: The Essential Writings and Speeches of Martin Luther King, Jr.* (New York: Harper Collins, 1991).

13. Tom Wells, *The War Within: America's Battle Over Vietnam* (Berkeley: University of California Press, 1994), pp. 223–402.

14. *The New Guard* 11, no. 5 (Summer 1971): 10–13.

15. Ibid., p. 12.

16. Ibid., pp. 12–13.

17. *Soldier of Fortune* started in 1976 with purple-prose stories about global mercenaries. Its early issues featured photographs of the mutilated bodies of African soldiers. Features about white male mercenaries freed of government control and interference were juxtaposed with articles on SWAT teams. Black urban neighborhoods became guerrilla zones where militarized police fought battles as their mercenary counterparts did in places like Africa and South America.

18. Gaines Smith, "How We Lost the 'War on Poverty,'" *The New Guard* 13, no. 5 (June 1973): 4–7. The history of OEO during the 1970s, and espe-

cially its controversial Community Action Program (CAP), demonstrated how the conservative agenda was beginning to transform American politics at a time when traditional liberal responses were confronted with grassroots challenges about how to affect poverty and racism. In 1970, Nixon put Howard Phillips, an archconservative, in charge of OEO, but after a bitter battle he was not confirmed and Donald Rumsfeld took charge. He turned to Dick Cheney for help and the task of redefining OEO. For interesting histories of this period and discussions of our social-welfare programs and philosophies, see Nancy A. Naples, *Grassroots Warriors: Activist Mothering, Community Work, and the War on Poverty* (New York: Routledge, 1998); Kenneth J. Neubeck and Noel A. Cazenave, *Welfare Racism: Playing the Race Card Against America's Poor* (New York: Routledge, 2001); Frances Fox Piven and Richard A. Cloward, *The Breaking of the American Social Compact* (New York: The New Press, 1997); and Barbara Cruikshank, *The Will to Empower: Democratic Citizens and Other Subjects* (Ithaca, NY: Cornell University Press, 1999).

19. Whitney M. Young, Jr., *Beyond Racism: Building an Open Society* (New York: McGraw-Hill, 1969). See also James Grossman, *Land of Hope: Chicago, Black Southerners, and the Great Migration* (Chicago: University of Chicago Press, 1989).

20. Michael K. Honey, *Southern Labor and Black Civil Rights: Organizing Memphis Workers* (Urbana: University of Illinois Press, 1993).

21. Kevin Boyle, *The UAW and the Heyday of American Liberalism, 1945–1968* (Ithaca, NY: Cornell University Press, 1995).

7. Riding the Reagan Highway

1. Edmund Morris, *Dutch: A Memoir of Ronald Reagan* (New York: Random House, 1999).

2. In the tumultuous 1976 Republican convention, language about the right to keep and bear arms was put into the Republican Platform by a conservative faction headed by Ronald Reagan. See also Robert Dallek, *Ronald Reagan and the Politics of Symbolism* (Cambridge, MA: Harvard University Press, 1984) and his *The Right Moment: Ronald Reagan's First Victory and the Decisive Turning Point in American Politics* (New York: Free Press, 2000).

3. Anon., "President Reagan's Speech Elicits Vigorous Applause," *The American Rifleman* 131, no. 7 (July 1983): 41.

4. Ibid., p. 40.

5. Ibid.

6. Ibid., p. 41.

7. The Civilian Marksmanship Program connected the members of the NRA with the 1903 National Board for the Promotion of Rifle Practice and its rhetorical legacy of the citizen-soldier in the militia and his in-training civilian counterpart. This training-in-arms and military-preparedness rationale had also justified the distribution of military surplus to civilians at minimal cost. Members of Congress have periodically challenged this policy. One period of conflict in the 1960s led to the 1966 Arthur D. Little Report by the Department of the Army that recommended the continuation of these programs. The report did mention in its major conclusions that the "recent Civil Rights directive issued by the DCM will result in improved control over those club memberships policies in order to insure compliance with Title VI of the Civil Rights Act," p. 84. It also concluded that "only a very small number of Negro or other nonwhites have applied for membership in DCM-affiliated clubs, especially in the South," p. 84. Whiteness continued to constitute a major factor in civilian rifle club membership. Quoted from the reproduction of the Arthur D. Little Report, in James B. Whisker, *The Citizen Soldier and United States Military Policy* (Croton-on-Hudson, NY: North River Press, 1979). In 1996, the Civilian Marksmanship Program was reorganized under the National Defense Authorization Act, making it a not-for-profit organization. See the Civilian Marksmanship Program website at http://www.odcmp.com, last accessed July 17, 2005. See also Robert J. Spitzer, *The Politics of Gun Control* (Washington, DC: CQ Press, 2004), pp. 76–78.

8. *The American Rifleman* 131, no. 7 (July 1983): 43.

9. *The Right to Keep and Bear Arms: Report of the Subcommittee on the Constitution of the Commitee on the Judiciary, United States Senate, Ninety-Seventh Congress, Second Session, February 1982* (Washington, DC: U.S. Government Printing Office, 1982).

10. Sixteen years later, in 1998, after the conservative Republican victories in Congress, the Second Amendment was again discussed in subcommittee. "Whose Right to Keep and Bear Arms? The Second Amendment as a Source of Individual Rights," Hearing Before the Subcommittee on the Constitution, Federalism, and Property Rights of the Committee on the Judiciary, United States Senate, One Hundred Fifth Congress, Second Session on Examining the Intent of the Second Amendment of the Constitution, Which Provides the Right to Keep and Bear Arms, September 23, 1998 (Washington, DC: U.S. Government Printing Office, 1999).

11. Susan Jeffords, *Hard Bodies: Hollywood Masculinity in the Reagan Era* (New Brunswick, NJ: Rutgers University Press, 1994).

12. The conservative repackaging of social ills under the framework of crime was predicted by Martin Luther King, Jr. He warned about how easy it would be for white America to exaggerate crime rather than face meaningful social change. In speaking of Goldwater's campaign for the presidency in 1964, King responded to the specter of a white backlash: see "Negroes Are Not Moving Too Fast," in James M. Washington, ed., *A Testament of Hope: The Essential Writings of Martin Luther King, Jr.* (New York: HarperCollins, 1991), p. 180.

13. The Firearms Owners' Protection Act of 1986, which is known as McClure-Volkmer, created a boom in gun shows because of the slippery concept of "doing business." As Robert J. Spitzer writes, the "act also eliminated record-keeping requirements for ammunition dealers, made it easier for individuals selling guns to do so without a license unless they did so 'regularly,' allowed gun dealers to do business at gun shows, and prohibited the ATF from issuing regulations requiring centralized records of gun dealers," in *The Politics of Gun Control*, p. 118.

14. In *Making a Killing: The Business of Guns in America* (New York: The New Press, 1999), Tom Diaz writes that, by 1970, the domestic handgun market had outpaced both the rifle and shotgun markets, p. 84. The periodic saturation of the market plagued the arms business in the United States. Diaz reported that the boom in handgun sales in the 1960s and '70s had already begun to taper off by 1984, p. 92. The need to have more advertising to drive sales became critical during this period when freedom was equated with gun ownership. See also the 2001 *National Gun Policy Survey*, conducted by the National Opinion Research Center, The University of Chicago, which reported the beginning of the decline of handgun sales to households in the 1990s. Also see "Firearms Commerce in the United States," Department of the Treasury, Bureau of Alcohol, Tobacco & Firearms, 2000 and 2001/2002 reports, which showed that the peak years for the manufacturing of pistols and revolvers were 1993 and 1994, with gradual declines thereafter. The report cautioned that these manufacturing figures do not literally reflect retail sales to individuals but seemed to indicate a trend to purchase before the Brady Law was passed in 1993 under the Clinton administration. See reports online at http://www.atf.treas.gov, last accessed August 5, 2005.

15. Diaz, *Making a Killing*, p. 47. Diaz also points out that nearly half of the guns available to civilians since the late nineteenth century were manufactured between 1974 and 1993, p. 69.

16. Ronald Reagan, *Reagan: A Life in Letters*, ed. Kiron K. Skinner, Annelise Anderson, and Martin Anderson (New York: Free Press, 2003), p. 55.

17. I am indebted to the discussion of this period in Lucy Mathiak and Lora Lumpe's "Government Gun-Running to Guerrillas," in Lora Lumpe, ed., *Running Guns: The Global Black Market in Small Arms* (London: Zed Books, 2000), pp. 55–80.

18. The Iran-Contra hearings document the Reagan-era drive to arm substate groups. See Lawrence E. Walsh, *Firewall: The Iran-Contra Conspiracy and Cover-Up* (New York: W. W. Norton, 1997); and Michael Lynch, *The Spectacle of History: Speech, Text, and Memory at the Iran-Contra Hearings* (Durham: Duke University Press, 1996).

19. Interestingly, the book on Gandhi that influenced many civil-rights workers in the United States was by Krishnalal Shridharani, *War Without Violence: A Study of Gandhi's Method and Its Accomplishments* (New York: Garland Publishing, Inc., 1972). In it, the tradition of *satyagraha* becomes central to action. Satyagraha simply means "insistence on truth," but Gandhi expanded the term to include direct action taken to confront massive injustice through nonviolence.

20. Carl Sandburg, *The Chicago Race Riots, July, 1919* (New York: Harcourt, Brace & World, 1969).

8. Deterrents

1. Confidential interview in October 2003.

2. John R. Lott, Jr., *More Guns, Less Crime: Understanding Crime and Gun-Control Laws* (Chicago: University of Chicago Press, 2000), pp. 164–65.

3. Kahn's concept of deterrence included three types and was as concerned with the first-strike capability of the United States, as with the acceptable risks of thermonuclear war, and survival after war. See Sharon Ghamari-Tabrizi, *The Worlds of Herman Kahn: The Intuitive Science of Thermonuclear War* (Cambridge, MA: Harvard University Press, 2005), pp. 46–60 and 202–35.

4. Herman Kahn, *On Thermonuclear War* (Westport, CT: Greenwood Press, 1969), pp. 126–60. Though in characteristic Kahn fashion, he also noted that "a purely military approach to the security problem can lead to disaster for civilization," p. 160. In the 1980s, Kahn spoke out again in reaction to Jonathan Schell's *The Fate of the Earth*, which critiqued the strategy of deterrence and advocated a rethinking of our political thought and institutions with a commitment to nuclear disarmament. Kahn wrote *Thinking About the Unthinkable in the 1980s* (New York: Simon &

Schuster, 1984) and attacked Schell's advocacy of a world government where national sovereignty relinquished some of its autonomy and self-determination for global security, pp. 207–24. For an interesting discussion of these issues in relationship to the Reagan years, see Frances FitzGerald, *Way Out There in the Blue: Reagan, Star Wars, and the End of the Cold War* (New York: Simon & Schuster, 2000).

5. Wayne LaPierre, *Guns, Crime, and Freedom* (New York: HarperPerennial, 1995), p. 28.

6. Editorial, "Veterans Day 1958," *The American Rifleman* 106, no. 11 (November 1958): 16.

7. Editorial, "Citizen Soldiers and Civil Defense," *The American Rifleman* 109, no. 12 (December 1961): 16.

8. "First Reports Evaluating the Effectiveness of Strategies for Preventing Violence: Firearms Laws," findings from the Task Force on Community Prevention Services, Centers for Disease Control, October 3, 2003, online recommendations at http//www.cdc.gov/mmwr, last accessed February 24, 2004. See also "Firearms and Violence: A Critical Review (2004)" by the Committee on Law and Justice, National Academy of Sciences, printed online by The National Academies Press at http://www.nap.edu/openbook/0309091241/html, last accessed August 5, 2005.

9. Ghamari-Tabrizi, *The Worlds of Herman Kahn*, p. 2.

10. Lott, *More Guns, Less Crime*, p. 3.

11. Ibid., p. 161.

12. Ibid., pp. 160–61.

13. Rich Roesler, "Group Seeks Vote on Required-Gun Measure," *The Spokesman-Review (Spokane)*, April 4, 1995. See City of Kennesaw, Georgia, Code of Ordinances & Gun Law at http://www.kennesaw.ga.us/CodeofOrdinances.aspx, last accessed February 22, 2004.

14. See the Morton Grove, Illinois, Library website on their handgun ordinance at http://www.webrary.org/ref/handgun.html, last accessed February 22, 2004.

9. Purchasing Power

1. Tom Diaz, *Making a Killing: The Business of Guns in America* (New York: The New Press, 1999), p. 49. Diaz writes that the "ATF estimates about two thousand of these shows," while the National Association of Arms Shows estimates "more than five thousand a year." James B. Jacobs, *Can Gun Control Work?* (New York: Oxford University Press, 2002), using later ATF data, states that in 1998 "there were 4,442 gun shows in the

United States, usually held in arenas, civic centers, fairgrounds, or armories. A gun show is typically a weekend event, drawing 2,500 to 5,000 attendees, who pay a small admission price to browse through the exhibits and examine and purchase firearms that catch their fancy," pp. 125–26. Also, federal law does define a gun show as a "function sponsored by any national, State, or local organization, devoted to the collection, competitive use, or other sporting use of firearms, or an organization or association that sponsors functions devoted to the collection, competitive use, or other sporting use of firearms in the community" (27 C.F.R. 178.100(b)). See the website of the Legal Community Against Violence online at http://www.lcav.org/content/mlgunshowsprint.asp, last accessed on February 20, 2006; see also "Gun Shows in America: Tupperware® Parties for Criminals," Violence Policy Center, 2000; and "GUNLAND USA: A State-by-State Ranking of Gun Shows, Gun Retailers, Machine Guns, and Gun Manufacturers," Violence Policy Center, 2000; and the 1999 Department of Treasury, Department of Justice, and Bureau of Alcohol, Tobacco and Firearms study, *Gun Shows: Brady Checks and Crime Gun Traces.*

2. Daren Briscoe, "Gun Show Suits Settled," *Los Angeles Times*, February 14, 2003, p. B1.

3. Gun-show organizers promote and coordinate the selling, buying, trading, and displaying of guns and gun accessories by collectors, gun clubs, private sellers, federally licensed dealers, gun-store dealers, and discount commercial dealers. These shows are open to the public and vary from state to state as to the restrictions placed upon buying weapons on the show premises. Gun-show organizers I have talked with have been owners of gun stores, coordinators of gun clubs, or businessmen associated with gun-rights groups who see an opportunity to collect in one place the diverse wares of gun owners and enthusiasts. A gun-show organizer can run several shows in a specific region and be connected with several local, state, and national associations that protect the interests of gun owners and gun-rights groups. See also *The Big Show Journal Magazine,* the Man at Arms Magazine National Gun Show Calendar, and the National Association of Arms Shows, Inc. In the state of Washington, major gun shows are organized by the Washington Arms Collectors. This group is affiliated with the NRA and has close local connections with the Gun Owners Action League of Washington, the Citizens Committee for the Right to Keep and Bear Arms, the Second Amendment Foundation, the Center for the Study of Firearms and Public Policy (which publishes

the *Journal of Firearms and Public Policy*), Talk America Radio Networks (which features a program called "Gun Talk"), and conservative property-rights groups like Wise Use. By "close connections" I mean not only over-lapping memberships, but even the sharing of office space and support staff.

4. David B. Kopel, "The Facts About Gun Shows," online at http://www .cato.org, last accessed on June 8, 2005.

5. When the Great Western gun show was faced with closure, its fight for survival was portrayed as a battle between Second Amendment free-doms and government interference. NRA staff ran a statewide mes-saging network to aid the embattled show. Anon., "NRA Helps the Great Western Gun Show, NRA Volunteers Help NRA," online at http://www.nrawinningteam.com/greatwestern/, last accessed on Aug-ust 7, 2005.

6. *Commerce in Firearms in the United States,* Department of the Treasury, Bureau of Alcohol, Tobacco & Firearms, February 2000, p. 6.

7. Tom Diaz, discusses the marketing techniques of gun manufacturers in *Making a Killing,* pp. 95–105. He quotes a manager of public relations at Smith & Wesson, who saw "a lot more advertising-driven buying," p. 95.

8. See Slavoj Zizek, *The Fragile Absolute, Or, Why Is the Christian Legacy Worth Fighting For?* (New York: Verso, 2001), and his *The Sublime Object of Ideology* (London: Verso, 1989).

9. David Hemenway, *Private Guns, Public Health* (Ann Arbor: University of Michigan Press, 2004), p. 36.

10. Ibid., p. 45.

11. Ibid., p. 36.

12. See *People, et. al. v. Arcadia Machine & Tool, Inc., et al.,* Declaration of Robert A. Ricker in Support of Plaintiffs' Opposition to Defendant Man-ufacturers' Motion for Summary Judgment, dated March 7, 2003, in the Superior Court of California, County of San Diego, Judicial Council Co-ordination Proceeding No. 4095. I would add, however, that Ricker still holds on to constitutional-right language to justify firearms ownership in the United States.

13. The NSSF runs the enormous SHOT show and, like the ASSC before it, promotes firearms as "American heritage." See Tom Diaz's discussion of trade association promoters in *Making a Killing,* pp. 50–68.

14. See Brian J. Siebel, "City Lawsuits Against the Gun Industry: A Roadmap For Reforming Gun Industry Misconduct," *St. Louis University Public Law Review* 18, no. 1 (1999): 247–90.

15. *Commerce in Firearms in the United States,* February 2000, has reported that "1.2 percent of dealers" accounted for "over 57 percent of the crime guns traced" in 1998.

16. Jordan Rau and Nancy Vogel, "Governor Signs Bill Banning .50–Calibers," *Los Angeles Times,* September 14, 2004, p. B4.

17. "Mission Statement," The Fifty Caliber Shooters Policy Institute, online at http://www.usa2076.com, last accessed on August 8, 2005. See also Fifty Caliber Shooters Association, online at http://www.fcsa.org, last accessed on August 8, 2005.

18. James William Gibson, *Warrior Dreams: Paramilitary Culture in Post-Vietnam America* (New York: Hill and Wang, 1994), pp. 265–97; and Susan Jeffords, *Hard Bodies: Hollywood Masculinity in the Reagan Era* (New Brunswick, NJ: Rutgers University Press, 1994). See also Diaz, *Making a Killing,* pp. 120–40, for advertising techniques.

19. Confidential interview on January 24, 2004.

20. Confidential interview on March 24, 2006.

21. Diaz, *The Business of Killing,* p. 69.

10. Gun-Grabbing Wives

1. Rev. Lawrence Shannon, *The Predatory Female: A Field Guide to Dating and the Marriage-Divorce Industry* (Reno, NV: Banner Books, Inc., 1997), p. ix.

2. For a discussion of domestic violence, see Ann Jones, *Next Time, She'll Be Dead: Battering and How to Stop It* (Boston: Beacon Press, 2000); Susan Schechter, *Women and Male Violence: The Visions and Struggles of the Battered Women's Movement* (Boston: South End Press, 1982); and Cheryl L. Sattler, *Teaching to Transcend: Educating Women Against Violence* (Albany: State University of New York Press, 2000). See federal law Section 922[g][8] of Title 18 of the United States Code and its discussion at the Office on Violence Against Women, Department of Justice, online at http://www.ojp.usdoj.gov, last accessed on February 26, 2004.

3. To get a sense of these legal issues, see H. Richard Uviller and William G. Merkel, *The Militia and the Right to Arms, Or, How the Second Amendment Fell Silent* (Durham, NC: Duke University Press, 2002), pp. 212–25.

4. Testimony given before the House Subcommittee on Crime by Ronald E. Hampton, online at the United States House of Representatives, Judiciary Committe website, http://www.house.gov/judiciary, last accessed on February 27, 2004. See also the testimony of Donna F. Edwards, execu-

tive director of the National Network to end Domestic Violence, at the same website.

5. Patricia Tjaden and Nancy Thoennes, "Prevalence, Incidence, and Consequences of Violence Against Women: Findings from the National Violence Against Women Survey," National Institute of Justice, Center for Disease Control and Prevention Research Brief, November 1998.

6. United States District Judge Sam R. Cummings, "Memorandum Opinion," in the United States District Court for the Northern District of Texas, San Angelo Division, *United States of America v. Timothy Joe Emerson*, Criminal Action No. 6:98–CR-103–C, online at http://www.txnd.uscourts.gov, last accessed on August 8, 2005.

7. This was especially true, the court found, since upon purchasing a Beretta semiautomatic pistol, the husband had signed a BAT Form 4473, stating that "so long as he was under a court order such as that of September 14, 1998, federal law prohibited his continued possession of that weapon." *United States v. Emerson* (No. 99-10331) (5th Cir. 2001).

8. Uviller and Merkel, *The Militia and the Right to Arms*, lists the groups submitting briefs for and against Emerson, p. 315, fn. 1. Besides the NRA, the Second Amendment Foundation, the Citizens Committee for the Right to Keep and Bear Arms, and the Texas State Rifle Association were among Emerson's supporters. Arguing against the Second Amendment interpretation were briefs filed by six groups, including the Center to Prevent Handgun Violence and the Domestic Violence Network.

9. The third judge on the court "choose not to join" in the lengthy individual-rights argument because they were "dicta" and "at best an advisory treatise on this long-running debate" and really had nothing to do with the decision made by the court. He went on to say that if the Second Amendment was interpreted as an individual and not a collective right, in a way, who cares? There would still be legal grounds for "reasonable restriction" on gun ownership.

11. Arming God's Nation

1. Confidential interview on January 14, 2004.

2. David A. Neiwert, *In God's Country: The Patriot Movement and the Pacific Northwest* (Pullman: Washington State University Press, 1999), pp. 11–12. See also Carolyn Gallaher, *On the Fault Line: Race, Class, and the American Patriot Movement* (Lanham, MD: Rowman & Littlefield, 2003) for a discussion of the militia in Kentucky.

3. John A. Andrew III, *The Other Side of the Sixties: Young Americans for Freedom and the Rise of Conservative Politics* (New Brunswick, NJ: Rutgers University Press, 1997), pp. 102–25.

4. "Shooting for Respectability: Firearms, False Patriots, and Politics in Montana," report issued by Montana Human Rights Network, Helena, MT, 2003, p. 30.

5. For a discussion of the rise of the new Christian Right, especially during and after the Reagan campaign for presidency, see Patrick Allitt, *Religion in America Since 1945: A History* (New York: Columbia University Press, 2003); Kenneth D. Wald, *Religion and Politics in the United States* (Lanham, MD: Rowman & Littlefield, 2003); and Gerald A. Almond, R. Scott Appleby, and Emmanuel Silvan, *Strong Religion: The Rise of Fundamentalisms Around the World (The Fundamentalism Project)* (Chicago: University of Chicago Press, 2003).

6. For a discussion of the dynamics of this transformation, especially during the Vietnam War years, see Amanda Porterfield, *The Transformation of American Religion: The Story of a Late-Twentieth-Century Awakening* (New York: Oxford University Press, 2001), pp. 88–124. See also Wade Clark Roof, *Spiritual Marketplace: Baby Boomers and the Remaking of American Religion* (Princeton, NJ: Princeton University Press, 1999).

7. See Benedict Anderson, *Imagined Communities: Reflections on the Origin and Spread of Nationalism* (London: Verso, 1991); and Nira Yuval-David, *Gender and Nation* (London: Sage Publications, 1997). Other writings on nationalism that address these issues are E. J. Hobsbawm, *Nations and Nationalism Since 1780: Programme, Myth, Reality* (New York: Cambridge University Press, 1990); and Ronald Beiner, ed., *Theorizing Nationalism* (Albany: State University of New York, 1999).

8. For a useful, but traditional, history of American religions, see Sydney E. Ahlstrom, *A Religious History of the American People* (New Haven, CT: Yale University Press, 2004).

9. Sitting in his prison cell in Italy, Antonio Gramsci wrote about what happened when a society was left primarily with police power or physical force to maintain its rule. The rise of powerful right-wing nationalist movements and the abuses of power under Fascism indicated to him that power obtained through consent was under assault. Shared values, or the perception and manipulation of shared values, what he called *cultural hegemony*, worked to build consent among the masses, and—for good and ill—created hierarchies of power that often turned against the very people who consented to them in the first place. And if that consent

weakened, physical force became the potent means to maintain the power structure. The threatening loss of consent through counter-hegemonic movements brought guns out in force. David Forgacs, ed., *The Antonio Gramsci Reader: Selected Writings 1916–1935* (New York: New York University Press, 2000), pp. 189–221.

10. Bernie Torrence, ed., "Principles of Proverbs," pamphlet for the Ministry of the International Fellowship of Christian Businessmen, St. Louis, Missouri.

12. Global Gun Grabbers

1. William Norman Grigg, *Global Gun Grab: The United Nations Campaign to Disarm Americans* (Appleton, WI: The John Birch Society, 2001).

2. See Chip Berlant and Matthew N. Lyons, *Right-Wing Populism in America: Too Close for Comfort* (New York: Guilford Press, 2000).

3. For an early study of these attitudes, see Gordon D. Hall, *The Hate Campaign Against the U. N.: One World Under Attack* (Boston: Beacon Press, 1952); for an early expression of them, see Gerald B. Winrod, *The United Nations: A Tower of Babel* (Wichita, KS: Defenders of the Christian Faith, 1953). For current conspiratorial rhetoric about the UN, see Tim LaHaye and Jerry B. Jenkins, *Left Behind: A Novel of the Earth's Last Days* (Wheaton, IL: Tyndale House Publishers, Inc., 1995) and its many sequels. Also see Robert W. Lee, *The United Nations Conspiracy* (Boston: Western Islands Publishers, 1981); and Jed Babbin, *Inside the Asylum* (Washington, DC: Regnery, 2004). For a more complex conservative analysis, see Dore Gold, *Tower of Babble: How the United Nations Fueled Global Chaos* (New York: Crown Forum, 2004).

4. Organizations like the NAACP initially advocated for more than civil rights for African Americans, fighting for an entire range of human rights such as education, health care, and economic justice. For an excellent analysis of how the NAACP after World War II pushed for human rights through the United Nations and was defeated by conservative and liberal forces in the United States, see Carol Anderson, *Eyes Off the Prize: The United Nations and the African American Struggle for Human Rights, 1944–1955* (New York: Cambridge University Press, 2003). The United Nations, with its Universal Declaration of Human Rights after the atrocities of World War II, contained ideas that challenged the economic interests of laissez-faire capitalism. For instance, Article 25, Section 1, states that "Everyone has the right to a standard of living adequate for the

health and well-being of himself and of his family, including food, clothing, housing and medical care and necessary social service, and the right of security in the event of unemployment, sickness, disability, widowhood, old age or other lack of livelihood in circumstances beyond his control." "Universal Declaration of Human Rights," online at http://www.un.org, last accessed on August 10, 2005. For a discussion of human rights, see Jack Donnelly, *Universal Human Rights in Theory and Practice* (Ithaca, NY: Cornell University Press, 2003).

5. They even take pride in claiming that members of the John Birch Society were active when the NRA grasped its political mission in 1977 and overthrew the old guard. In 1998, William F. Jasper wrote in *The New American* that at the fateful 1977 NRA annual meeting in Cincinnati, "JBS members who were voting delegates helped lead and coordinate a dramatic coup in which all the plotters—NRA officers Garcelon, Rich, Reynolds, Gutermuth, and Billings—were sacked on the spot. The plans to convert the organization into a 'Sierra Club with guns' were also scuttled." *The New American* 14, no. 25 (December 7, 1998): 10, online at http://www.thenewamerican.com, last accessed on May 30, 2005. See also the John Birch Society article by R. D. Patrick Mahoney, "The N.R.A. Backfire," *The Review of the NEWS*, April 13, 1977, pp. 1–5.

6. "The Gottlieb-Tartaro Report," Issue 041 (May 1998): 1, online at http://www.saf.org, last accessed on May 31, 2005.

7. Virginia Gamba, *Small Arms in Southern Africa: Reflections on the Extent of the Problem and Its Management Potential*, Monograph No. 42, November 1999, Institute for Security Studies.

8. "The G8 and Small Arms," *Ploughshares Monitor*, June 1998, online at http://www.ploughshares.ca, last accessed on June 1, 2005.

9. "Report of the United Nations Conference on the Illicit Trade in Small Arms and Light Weapons in All Its Aspects," New York, 9–10 July 2001 (New York: United Nations, 2001) presents a timetable of "initiatives undertaken at the regional and sub regional levels to address the illicit trade in small arms and light weapons," pp. 17–22.

10. See Albright's speech on Small Arms Control online at http://secretary.state.gov/www/statements/1998/980924.html, last accessed on July, 2005.

11. Representatives of organizations such as the International Alliance for Women, Million Mom March, Oxfam, Amnesty International, Federation of American Scientists, and Human Rights Watch attended, as did representatives of the National Rifle Association and Safari International.

12. Quoted in Kathi Austin, "Jesse Helms & the NRA Take Their Version of the Second Amendment Global," *Washington Post*, May 26, 2000.

13. Over the last thirty years, global women's issues have influenced structure and policymaking at the United Nations, raising questions about the traditional political and policy approaches of the United States and other developed nations. See Arvonne S. Fraser and Irene Tinker, *Developing Power: How Women Transformed International Development* (New York: The Feminist Press at the City University of New York, 2004).

14. Statement by John R. Bolton, United States Under Secretary of State for Arms Control and International Security Affairs, to the Plenary Session of the UN Conference on the Illicit Trade in Small Arms and Light Weapons in all its Aspects, July 9, 2001, online at http://www.un.int .usa/01_104.htm, last accessed on May 31, 2005. To read Ashcroft's letter to the NRA, see a copy online at the Violence Policy Center, http://www.vpc.org, last accessed on May 31, 2005.

15. For instance, lethal weapons such as the .50 caliber rifle, specific assault rifles, and semiautomatic weapons that can be converted to fully automatic weapons cross over categories from military to domestic.

16. Lora Lumpe, ed., *Running Guns: The Global Black Market in Small Arms* (New York: Zed Books, 2000); and Tom Diaz, *Making a Killing: The Business of Guns in America* (New York: The New Press, 1999), pp. 69–105. See also Lora Lumpe and Jeff Donarski, *The Arms Trade Revealed: A Guide for Investigators and Activists* (Washington, DC: Federation of American Scientists Fund, 1998).

17. "Review of U.S. Participation in UNESCO: Hearings and Markup Before the Subcommittee on International Operations, and on Human Rights and International Organizations of the Committee on Foreign Affairs," House of Representatives, Ninety-seventh Congress, March 10, July 9 and 16, 1981 (Washington, DC: U.S. Government Printing Office, 1982) and "U.S. Withdrawal from UNESCO: A Report of a Staff Study Mission," February 10–23, 1984, to the Committee on Foreign Affairs, U.S. House of Representatives (Washington, DC: U.S. Government Printing Office, 1984). See also Garry Wills, *Reagan's America* (New York: Penguin Books, 1988), p. 353.

18. Rep. Ron Paul, "American Sovereignty Restoration Act of 2003." To read the act, its summary, and major actions, see http://thomas.loc.gov, last accessed on May 30, 2005.

19. Online at http://www.house.gov/paul/congrec/congrec2003/cr091803.htm, last accessed on February 13, 2006.

20. For a discussion of how women have become an active part of the culture-of-peace movement, see Ingeborg Breines, Dorota Gierycz, and Betty A. Reardon, eds., *Towards a Women's Agenda for a Culture of Peace* (Paris: UNESCO Publishing, 1999).

21. In 1999, a coalition of civil society organizations launched The Hague Appeal for Peace, an ambitious project for those "concerned with peace and disarmament, human rights, indigenous peoples' rights, gender, the environment, faith-based approaches, peace education and youth." See The Hague Appeal for Peace and Justice for the 21st Century, online at http://www.unesco.org, last accessed on May 30, 2005. The challenge presented at the conference was to think outside the box of nationalism. "It is time to redefine security in terms of human and ecological needs instead of national sovereignty and national borders. Redirecting funds from armaments to human security and sustainable development will establish new priorities leading to the construction of a new social order which ensures the equal participation of marginalized groups, including women and indigenous people, restricts use of military force, and moves toward collective global security." For a general discussion of the culture of peace, see David Adams, ed., *UNESCO and A Culture of Peace* (Paris: UNESCO Publishing, 1997). For critiques of the concept and the problems of human security through United Nations initiatives, see Michael N. Barnett and Martha Finnemore, *Rules for the World: International Organizations in Global Politics* (Ithaca, NY: Cornell University Press, 2004); and David Rieff, *At the Point of a Gun: Democratic Dreams and Armed Intervention* (New York: Simon & Schuster, 2005).

22. Grigg, *Global Gun Grab*, p. 51.

23. The John Birch Society differed from other conservative groups who strongly supported both the militarization of the police and increased military spending at the Pentagon. For the JBS, the only justification for military action was to fight off Communist threats both within and outside the United States, and in that one gesture they rearmed both the civilian and military forces to restrain whomever they designated as subversive to the American way.

24. The Woman's Portal at the International Action Network on Small Arms (IANSA) tracks many of the activities of grassroots and national organizations seeking gun regulation. Also, the Canadian criminologist Wendy Cukier asserts that in 1997, the NRA began to support gun-lobbying efforts in eleven countries and has provided consultants and supported public-relations campaigns in Canada, Japan, the United Kingdom, and

South Africa. With Victor W. Sidel, she has written *The Global Gun Epidemic: From Saturday Night Specials to AK-47s* (Westport, CT: Praeger Security International, 2006). See also Kelly Hearn, "As Brazil Votes to Ban Guns, NRA Joins in the Fight," *The Nation,* November 7, 2005, online at http://www.thenation.com/doc/20051107/hearn, last accessed on February 13, 2006.

INDEX